S0-ESG-679

MICHIGAN STATE UNIVERSITY LIBRARIES
AUG 14 2025
WITHDRAWN

PLACE IN RETURN BOX to remove this checkout from your record.
TO AVOID FINES return on or before date due.

DATE DUE	DATE DUE	DATE DUE
NOV 05 2012		

MSU Is An Affirmative Action/Equal Opportunity Institution
c:\circ\datedue.pm3-p.1

AGEING AND OLD AGE

AGEING AND OLD AGE
among Chinese in a Singapore urban neighbourhood

KUA EE HEOK
MBBS (Mal), MD (S'pore), FRCPsych (U.K.), FAMS

Department of Psychological Medicine
National University of Singapore

SINGAPORE UNIVERSITY PRESS
NATIONAL UNIVERSITY OF SINGAPORE

©1994 Singapore University Press
Kent Ridge, Singapore 0511

All rights reserved

ISBN 9971-69-185-X (Paper)

HQ
1064
.S55
K822
1994

Typeset and printed by: Eazi Printing Pte Ltd

CONTENTS

FOREWORD — vii
ACKNOWLEDGEMENTS — ix

Chapter One : Whys and wherefores — 1

Chapter Two : Social landscape — 5

Chapter Three : Life after sixty-five — 11

Chapter Four : The mind in old age — 25

Chapter Five : Physical health — 43

Chapter Six : Drinking habits — 48

Chapter Seven : The old-old — 51

Chapter Eight : Elderly men and women — 55

Chapter Nine : The elderly in Singapore and the United States — 58

Chapter Ten : The future elderly — 62

APPENDIX I — 68
REFERENCES — 71
INDEX — 80

FOREWORD

In Singapore it has been projected that by the turn of the year 2000, the number of elderly aged 60 years and over will increase significantly. Although the annual growth rate of the ageing population for the next 40 years will be around 3%, it is assessed that percentage increase will be more accelerated between 1990 to 2005. The elderly population will grow between 14% and 26% from 1990 to 2010. Such a sharp increase will have serious implications to services for the elderly. More importantly the number of "old-old" persons 75 years and above will see a steep increase. This group is at high risk for care and attention. More family resources will have to be drawn to attend to their social and physical requirements and some families would face stress and or problems to provide care for the aged sick and disabled. These observations and demographic changes are highlighted by Professor Kua Ee Heok in this book. The book also introduces readers to some specific issues confronting our ageing population and the author's effort producing this publication is indeed commendable.

In older housing estates, the ageing process has become more transparent. There are increasing numbers of older senior citizens living in these estates and it is urgent that community groups and organisations begin to plan the establishment of more community-based programmes such as day care, meals programmes, home-help services and domicilary nursing care and crisis response service. In taking a proactive approach to initiate a network of services in older housing estates, we will be able to provide support for families with vulnerable aged and prevent disruptions to the social and economic lives of the families.

One major concern facing the elderly would be the maintenance of good health. It is therefore important to promote healthy living. Otherwise ill health at old age can become burdensome and a misery. The prolongation of live as a result of improved medical technology would raise various moral and philosophical issues about sustenance of life and dying. Our elderly will have to be better prepared to deal with this life reality and dilemma. For the elderly to reduce risk against disabling conditions, it is important to enhance their physical and mental capacities and strengthen their support networks. Readers will find that these important aspects are adequately covered in this book.

Our community must take steps to encourage our elderly to be better prepared to cope with their retirement. The more positive efforts the elderly take in maintaining healthy life styles, the less dependent they will be in need for care and attention. We must therefore motivate more of our elderly to be involved in self-help groups in our neighbourhoods. Through these self-help groups and mutual support groups, the elderly with different needs and problems could be assisted. The strong can help the less strong.

I hope that Professor Kua Ee Heok's book on *Ageing and Old Age* will help to stimulate interest among various community groups to take steps to tackle the challenges facing a growing ageing population in Singapore. His publication will hopefully prod the conscience of our community to organise more help for the aged sick. I am sure that those working in the field of gerontology will be pleased with an additional local publication on ageing issues and they will be inspired further by the author's view points to develop new programmes to meet emerging needs of our ageing population, particularly those at risk.

Dr S Vasoo
Head, Department of Social Work & Psychology
National University of Singapore
1993

ACKNOWLEDGEMENTS

This book is, in essence, a synopsis of a dissertation submitted to the National University of Singapore for the degree of Doctorate of Medicine. From the primordial stage of the preparation to the final draft, I have been encouraged and assisted by the following for whom I am profoundly grateful.

Professor John Copeland from the Department of Psychiatry, University of Liverpool, England, provided invaluable guidance on the research. Associate Professor James Lee, from the Department of Community, Occupational and Family Medicine, National University of Singapore, advised on statistical analysis of data. Professor Scott Henderson, National Health and Medical Research Council, Social Psychiatry Research Unit, The Australian National University, gave suggestion on methodology.

I also wish to thank Dr. S. Vasoo, Head, Department of Social Work & Psychology, National University of Singapore, for writing the foreword. He is also the Member of Parliament of the constituency where the research was conducted.

Finally, I am indebted to Ms T. Vanaja for secretarial assistance and Ms Kua Yu Sim who read the manuscript and gave helpful comments.

1

WHYS AND WHEREFORES

One is often inspired to embark on a research by the realisation that there is a gap in the general body of knowledge. It is often this inspiration which generates the enthusiasm and energy to sustain the long odyssey of the research. I have been intrigued by the numerous studies on the elderly in the developed countries and how often these results have been extrapolated to the developing countries. The validity of the extrapolation has to be tested, and indeed some assumptions have been proven to be fallacious. Do cultural and socio-economic factors influence ageing and the perception of health and illness? Some questions seem rhetorical at face value, but it is obviously necessary to probe deeper into the issues.

Research on the elderly has expanded immensely in the last two decades, in tandem with the greying of the population in the developed countries. One of the most vigorous and impressive gerontological studies is the longitudinal survey of elderly Americans in Durham, North Carolina. This massive epidemiological research has yielded valuable information on ageing in America, and much have also been learned on the methodology (Duke OARS 1978). The cross-national study on dementia and depression between New York and London is an important milestone in international research which has helped to broaden our horizon on geriatric psychiatry (Gurland *et al.* 1983). In the east, Japan has set the impetus for gerontological research and data gathering on the Asian elderly (Hasegawa 1974). Unfortunately there is a dearth of information from the developing countries to allow for comparison. For cross-national comparison to be possible, there must be a common research instrument or questionnaire, uniform criteria of diagnoses and acceptable methodology.

A cause of global concern is the rapidity of ageing of the population in the developing countries. Guatemala heads the list with Singapore second, according to the UN Bureau of Census (UN 1987). The speed of the demographic change is alarming because of its social and economic implications. For example, who will provide for the elderly, what services are needed, how will the economy be affected and what about future trend? Developing countries often encounter difficulties in planning services and programmes because of a scarcity of local statistics. The United Nation classifies countries as 'aged' if the proportion of people in their populations who are 65 or older is 7% or more. It is predicted that in the next 30 years nearly all nations of the world will reach the 7% mark.

In Singapore, there is an increasing concern about the growing proportion of elderly people. In 1970 only 3% of the population was 65 years and more (Table 1.1). By 1980 this had increased to 5% and in the year 2000 the proportion will have risen to 8%. There will be an accelerated pace in the twenty-first century and the projected figure for 2030 is a fifth of the total population. Comparing the two subgroups of elderly people, the proportion of 'young-old' (65 to 74 years) will decline from 78% in 1987 to 76% in 2000 and 71% in 2030, but the 'old-old' (75 years and above) will increase from 22% in 1987 to 24% in 2000 and 29% in 2030 (Table 1.2). Therefore within the elderly population, there is in fact a proportional increase in the 'old-old' and a decrease in the 'young-old'.

Table 1.1: Population of Singapore 1970-2030
(in thousands)

Age Group	Year			
	1970	1980	2000	2030
0 - 14	804.8 (39%)	635.1 (27%)	671.1 (22%)	574.4 (18%)
15 - 64	1200.3 (58%)	1646.8 (68%)	2103.3 (70%)	2000.5 (62%)
65 & above	69.4 (3%)	113.9 (5%)	220.7 (8%)	639.1 (20%)
Total	2075 (100%)	2414 (100%)	2995 (100%)	3214 (100%)

Source: Population Planning Unit, Ministry of Health, 1982.

Table 1.2: Estimated Elderly Population of Singapore 1987-2030
(in thousands)

Age Group	1987	Year 2000	2030
65 - 74	96 (78%)	141 (76%)	396 (71%)
75 & above	46 (22%)	79 (24%)	242 (29%)
Total	142 (100%)	220 (100%)	638 (100%)

Source: Population Planning Unit, Ministry of Health, 1982.

The greying of the population in Singapore is mainly due to a decline in the fertility rate, which fell dramatically in the last decade as a result of a successful family planning campaign. The emphasis on small family has altered the demographic structure. The consequence is fewer children to look after their elderly parents. Other factors include the decline in the mortality rate and the change in life expectancy, which has increased progressively from 50 years in 1947 to 72 years for men and 74 years for women in 1988. These changes are due to advances in medical sciences eliminating many diseases, improvement of public health services, better care of infants and children, better nutrition, and a more healthy life style.

The demographic trend in Singapore has prompted the appointment of a Ministerial Committee "to study the problems of the increasing number of aged people in our population and their consequences to our society and to recommend measures to prevent, ameliorate or deal with such problems" (Ministry of Social Affairs 1983). Beyond any doubt, unless there are basic facts and figures to buttress hypothesis, all planning and boardroom discussion will become a mere exercise in futility. The Ministerial Committee commissioned a national survey of senior citizens and a report published in May 1983 (Ministry of Social Affairs 1983). The survey encompassed a wide scope including family life, finance, health care, activities of daily living and employment. Under health care, the section on mental health was inadequately surveyed. This could be because the survey was expansive and it would be difficult to cover any one section thoroughly. Moreover, the survey was conducted by lay investigators who could only elicit symptoms but not diagnose. One major drawback of this survey was that, unfortunately, no standardised research instrument or questionnaire was used and this handicapped any international comparison.

There is a compelling need for a comprehensive study on the health and care of elderly people living in the community. What is their functional status, social life and support system? The data can provide seminal information for rational health services planning and policy formulation. An epidemiological study in the community yields useful results but a biased sample in an institutional home only serves to reinforce the misconception of decrepitude of elderly people. The national survey by the Ministry of Social Affairs (1983) had adequate information on financial resource, and therefore this enquiry was omitted in this study.

The objectives of the research were:
1. To study the social characteristics of a random sample of elderly people living in the community.
2. To ascertain their social resources and family care.
3. To examine their physical and mental health.
4. To compare the functional status of:
    i. the young-old and old-old.
    ii. elderly men and women.

This book presents research data on the elderly in the Chinese districts of Tiong Bahru, Bukit Merah and Henderson of Singapore. What is the good news about ageing? How do elderly people perceive old age? How is life after sixty-five? What are their health problems and who care for them? These are some of the questions on ageing and old age, which are *sine qua non* for future planning of programmes and needs of elderly people in Singapore.

2

SOCIAL LANDSCAPE

Selecting a random sample for an epidemiological research is always a problem. Can a sample be indeed representative of the population at large? The answer can never be 'yes'. In a plural society like Singapore, the variables for stratification are numerous besides sex and age, there are religion, ethnicity, education, employment, etc. As about 78% of Singaporeans live in public housing flats, it will not be inappropriate to focus on the elderly in these housing estates, although this may mean that the affluent elderly in private accommodations will be excluded. In the main, the estates are not homogenous, some are older, others poorer or have a greater proportion of elderly or young residents. A random selection may include an estate with only a few elderly and for the time invested and energy expended, the yield could be meagre.

This study was confined to three predominantly Chinese constituencies at Tiong Bahru, Bukit Merah and Henderson. The districts were selected mainly because of their proximity to the Singapore General Hospital and because there are two elderly day centres in the Henderson district. Subjects for the research could be assessed in the day centres and further laboratory investigations conducted in the Singapore General Hospital.

The Tiong Bahru constituency borders the old Chinatown and the ethnic composition is Chinese 86%, Malays 7% and Indians 5%. Elderly people, 65 years and more, comprise 9% of the citizenry of 18,500. The majority of residents are from social class III or IV and work as clerks, technicians, hawkers, etc. There are many different criteria to define what is social class and a common classification is based on occupation (Table 2.1). There are inherent problems in this widely accepted classification because the interpretation of skilled and semi-skilled occupations can sometimes be ambiguous, and even between semi-skilled and unskilled. To minimise ambiguity, social classes IV and V are combined in the analysis. Most elderly people were retired and classification would be based on previous occupation. For housewives, classification was according to their husband's occupations.

The Henderson constituency is north of Tiong Bahru and has a population of 20,000 with 8% elderly and an ethnic ratio similar to Tiong Bahru. Compared to the other two constituencies, the residents of Henderson are by and large poorer — mainly social class IV or V. Many work in Chinatown as shop assistants, labourers or hawkers. The Bukit Merah or Redhill constituency is adjacent to Henderson and derives its name from the red clay of five hills which once dominated the panorama. It has a population of 20,200 with Chinese 82%, Malays 10% and Indians 6%; the elderly constitute about 9% of the population. These three constituencies have a greater proportion of elderly people than others in Singapore.

Table 2.1: Hierarchy of Social Class

Social Class	Occupation
I	Professional, manager, landowner
II	Intermediate occupation, e.g. nurses, social workers, teachers
III	Skilled occupation
IV	Semi-skilled occupation
V	Unskilled occupation

The Election Department in the National Registration Office maintains a record of Singapore identity card holders in every electoral constituency. The Election Department was contacted in May 1985 and a random sample of 1000 elderly Chinese 65 years and more was selected from the electoral roll. The selection of persons was based on a stratified random sample and the variables for stratification were sex and age. The sampling procedure ensured that each age group and sex was proportionally represented as in the 1980 census of population.

The study was conducted from July to December 1985. Initial contacts with the subjects in their homes were made by a nurse, who had previous experience working with the elderly. Sometimes she had to make two or three home visits because the subjects could be away at work, visiting friends, shopping or in hospital. If after the third visit the person was not present, then this would be classified as 'not contactable'. The nurse also arranged for an appointment for a health assessment by the author at the Apex Day Centre or the Henderson Social Centre. Twenty-five subjects were unable to go to the day centres because of illness and had to be examined in their homes. Of the original sample of 1000 subjects only 612 were interviewed (Table 2.2). The nurse was unable to contact 127 subjects because many of them had left home for work at 8.00 a.m. and returned late at night.

The health assessment consisted of an interview using a semi-structured questionnaire and a physical examination. In the initial interview, the nurse inquired about personal data, activities of daily living (ADL) and social resources. Activities of daily living measure levels of independence in basic everyday activities and the social resources questionnaire examines relationships with family and friends. The rating scales for ADL, social resources and physical health are adapted from the Older American Resources and Services schedule (Duke OARS 1978). This is a comprehensive assessment schedule for the rating of functional status of the elderly and has been widely used in international gerontological research. For mental health assessment, the Geriatric Mental State (GMS) schedule constructed by Copeland *et al.* (1976), was used. The GMS is a semi-structured standardised interview instrument developed by the Anglo-American team in the London-New York study on the elderly (Copeland *et al.* 1976, Gurland *et al.* 1976). Since its introduction, the GMS has been used in research in the United Kingdom, the United States, Australia and Europe. In Singapore, a pilot study using the GMS showed good validity and reliability.

Table 2.2: Sample of Elderly Subjects

	Number
Total sample	1000
Deceased	23
Hospitalised	10
Returned to China	18
Shifted residence	116
Not contactable	127
Refused to be interviewed	31
No such persons	47
*Others e.g. incorrect address, wrong date of birth	16
Interviewed	612

* Including 3 Indians and 7 Malays.

Profile of Sample

To allow for comparison of different strata of age groups, the subjects were divided into two groups 65 to 74 years (young-old), and 75 and more (old-old). As shown in Table 2.3, the sample interviewed reflected closely the proportion of elderly people in the 1980 census of population. About two thirds of the sample were the young-olds and one third old-olds. The mean age of the former group was 69 years and the latter 78 years. There was a slight preponderance of women (55%) over men (45%) and this was similar to the 1980 census (Table 2.4). The ratio of men to women was almost similar in the young-old but in the old-old there was a higher proportion of women.

Analysis of the marital status showed that in the young-old, 7% were single, 56% married, 35% widowed and 2% divorced or separated. In the old-old, 10% were single, 33% married, 56% widowed and 1% divorced or separated (Table 2.5). The proportions of single and divorced or separated were quite similar in both age groups but more in the old-old group were widowed.

Table 2.3: Age Distribution of Sample

Age Group	1980 Census	Sample
65 - 74	82,630 (72%)	432 (71%)
75 & more	31,270 (28%)	180 (29%)
Total	113,900 (100%)	612 (100%)

Table 2.4: Age and Sex Distribution

Age Group	Men	Women	Total
65 - 74	209 (48%)	223 (52%)	432 (100%)
75 & more	69 (38%)	111 (62%)	180 (100%)
Total	78 (45%)	334 (55%)	612 (100%)

Table 2.5: Marital Status

Age Group	Single	Married	Widowed	Divorced/separated	Total
65 - 74	30 (7%)	242 (56%)	153 (35%)	7 (2%)	432 (100%)
75 & above	17 (10%)	60 (33%)	101 (56%)	2 (1%)	180 (100%)
Total	47 (8%)	302 (49%)	254 (42%)	9 (1%)	612 (100%)

In the sample, only 14% of young-olds and 11% of old-olds were in social class I and II (Table 2.6). The majority of elderly people in the three constituencies belonged to social class IV and V — 70% in the young-olds and 71% in the old-olds. Occupation is often a reflection of educational status. About 57% of the sample, mainly from social class IV and V had no education, 34% primary, 8% secondary and 1% tertiary education. The demographic data on age, sex and marital status of the sample reflect closely the elderly population in Singapore; but certainly the social class status is not representative. One would expect a normal curve spread rather than a skewed distribution for social class with a preponderance of social class IV and V.

Table 2.6: Social Class

Age Group	I	II	III	IV and V	Total
65 - 74	13 (3%)	48 (11%)	70 (16%)	301 (70%)	432 (100%)
75 & above	5 (3%)	15 (8%)	33 (18%)	127 (71%)	180 (100%)
Total	16 (3%)	63 (10%)	103 (17%)	428 (70%)	612 (100%)

About a third of the sample were immigrants from the southern Chinese provinces of Kwangtung and Fujian. They came to Singapore to seek employment before and soon after the Second World War. They worked in a myriad of semi-skilled and unskilled jobs in Chinatown and the port as shopkeepers, hawkers, clerks, domestic servants, stevedores, bumboatmen, labourers, etc. But there were also skilled workers, e.g. artisans for the building industry, teachers, craftmen, etc. Many of these migrant workers had no intention of settling down in Singapore and wanted only, as many confided, "to make enough money and go back to our village in China to buy a piece of land or start a business". But the communist victory in China after the war obliterated that dream, and they could not return to their homeland. However, the political changes in China in the last decade have made it possible for many to return. Many immigrants succeeded in scaling to a higher social status, but others lingered on the lower rungs of the hierarchy. The noveau riche resettled in the fashionable quarters of Singapore away from Chinatown, but the less successful had to resign themselves to the enclaves of dingy overcrowded accommodation around Chinatown. The shift of the wealthy away from this district could have contributed to the skewed distribution of social class in the sample.

3

LIFE AFTER SIXTY-FIVE

In his book, *The View in Winter*, Ronald Blythe (1972) made insightful observations about ageing in an English village. He noticed that there were two groups of elderly people in the village — those who grew up there (the locals) and those who came from the city to retire (the immigrants). A similar trend is observed in Singapore in the housing estates. The majority of the elderly in the study lived within or at the periphery of Chinatown since childhood — they were the locals. But in recent years, with urban redevelopment and industrial growth sprouting around Bukit Merah, there had been an influx of immigrant elderly who followed their children to resettle here. The local elderly had lived together in the same environs for many years and consequently had a sense of camaraderie. They could be seen in the void decks of flats, coffee shops or community centres, playing chess, having a desultory conversation or listening to the 'merbok' (song-birds). Even today such coalescence of elderly people is often based on dialect and clan kinship. Cantonese dialect enclaves are scattered around the Henderson district, with more Teochew in Tiong Bahru and Hokkien in Bukit Merah.

The 'immigrant' elderly had been uprooted from their previous entrenched milieu, and could encounter adjustment difficulties in alien territory. Unlike the immigrant elderly in the English village, who preferred the solitude of rural life, these elderly did not move on their own accord. Adaptation is easier for young people, who are able to seek companionship at their work place. But it can be problematic for the elderly, who may feel socially sequestered and often become marooned in their flats. An ex-carpenter told me, "I don't even know who my neighbour is. Everybody locks the door." A retired farmer, who was 'transplanted' to Henderson district because of his son's job, said that he could not brook the 'culture shock' of living in a congested high-rise building and would make weekly bus trip back to his village in Woodlands to visit old friends or coterie. He found it difficult to 'break into' the inner circle of the local elderly and he felt as if he was an alien in a different subculture.

Perception of Old Age

An intriguing question in gerontology is the onset of old age. Could this be at 55, 65 or even 70? Undeniably, there is no temporal watershed between middle age and old age. The chronological age is certainly not a good benchmark and the biological age which has to do with physical changes like hair colour, skin texture and sensory acuity, differs with every individual. Indeed a feeling of growing old is subjective and personal. There are many psychological and social factors which may influence perception of old age. In ancient China, being 60 was considered old and because of the reverence for the elderly, people looked forward to it. According to Chinese tradition, from the age of 60 a person begins to acquire dignity and he is entitled to carry a staff in his village, at 70 he is entitled to carry a staff in the country, at 80 he is entitled to carry a staff before the emperor (Lee 1987). But in a society that worships youth and disparages old people, there is less inclination to accept old age. Another factor is the person's attitude toward life and ageing. A positive attitude recognises the advantages and disadvantages in growing old. It is an axiom that people who remain active — physically and mentally — in late life are less likely to feel old. But usually the transition from middle age to old age is gradual and passes by imperceptibly. Retirement has an enormous impact on the psyche of workers — it means, to many, the harbinger of old age. Previously when the retirement age was 50, people who were 50 felt old. Today it has shifted upwards to 60 and the 55 consider themselves as young. Therefore, the meaning of old age varies with needs and attitudes.

In this survey, the elderly subjects were asked when they first began to feel old. Table 3.1 illustrates their responses — 76% indicated that it was 60 years or more and 52%, 65 years or more; however there was no sex difference. Cross-analysis of the results shows that the 24% who suggested 50 to 59 years were mainly those elderly who had physical illness; and those 30% who mentioned 70 years and more were the healthy elderly. An interesting finding is that only 16% of those who were still working — compared with 36% of those not working — felt that the onset of ageing commenced between 50-59 years. With such wide variation, it can be concluded that the official definition of old age is different from the individual person's experience

A related question was about what they experienced were the signs of early ageing. About 60% said that it was a change of visual acuity or hearing difficulty, 11% mentioned poor memory, 22% slow movement due to arthritis and 7% medical illness, e.g. heart diseases, diabetes mellitus, etc. It seems that a powerful determinant of perception of ageing is health status.

Table 3.1: Perception of Old Age

Perceived onset of old age (in years)	Percentage of sample (n=612)
50 - 54	11%
55 - 59	13%
60 - 64	24%
65 - 69	22%
70 and above	30%
Total	100%

An item in the questionnaire explored life satisfaction: 'Taking everything into consideration, what is your satisfaction with life in general'. This broad question which is an indicator of successful ageing, covers past and present situations. About 72% were very satisfied, 23% fairly satisfied and 5% dissatisfied — there was no difference between men and women (Table 3.2). Those who were satisfied gave their reasons: good family 41%, physical comfort 29% (e.g. house, refrigerator, cooker, car, etc.), good health 23% and others 7% (e.g. holidays in China). A greater proportion of those living with their families (70%), compared with those who lived alone (45%) expressed satisfaction. Dissatisfaction was because of: poor health 54%, family conflict 30%, financial problems 13%, others 3% (e.g. caring for sick relatives). This once again underscores the fact that one of the major preoccupations in late life is health. The majority of the dissatisfied elderly were in poor health and a high proportion of those satisfied mentioned about their good health. A cliche they often pontificated was "you can't enjoy retirement in sickness". Even in the United Kingdom, health status has been found to be a powerful predictor of life satisfaction (Bowling 1991).

One of the features of life satisfaction is adjustment in old age. Those who are well adjusted often look to the future with interest and look back with satisfaction. They are realistic about the limitations of age and accepts the inevitability of death without fear. But the maladjusted perceive ageing and disabilities with angst. They tend to be resentful, bitter about the past and pessimistic of the future.

Life satisfaction correlates well with the theories of 'activity' versus 'disengagement' during retirement. The proponents of the 'activity' theory argue that since old age is often associated with loss and diminished relationship, activity may be necessary for social integration and expanding social network. But this hinges on many factors including health status, personality and family support. A frail elderly may loath to be involved but is contented with minimal family interaction. An extrovert and gregarious person may need to channel his enthusiasm in community service, but an introvert would prefer the solitude of his garden. Continuation of previous life style may be more difficult in old age; the maintenance of some interactions and activities could be essential for life satisfaction. The 'disengagement' theory posits successful ageing as a processes of progressive detachment from active participation in roles, e.g. job, family life and organisation. Gradual withdrawal from responsibilities is necessary but total disengagement may not be the best counsel. In short, adherence of extreme in both theories is to be eschewed.

Table 3.2: Life Satisfaction

	Percentage of Sample (n=612)
Excellent	11%
Good	61%
Fair	23%
Poor	4%
Very poor	1%
Total	100%

Social Resources

The living arrangement of the elderly in the study is shown in Table 3.3. Over 80% were living with their family members, i.e. spouse or children. Only 5% of young-old and 7% of old-old were living alone. Another 9% of the young-old and 12% of old-old were living with friends. There is no apparent difference between the two groups. For those with families, 63% were living with sons, 19% daughters, 12% spouse and 6% other relatives. The family provides not only emotional support and care in illness but also financial assistance. Those living with friends or alone were mainly the unmarried elderly and less commonly, the widowed. There was no difference in living arrangement between elderly men and women.

Table 3.3: Living Arrangement

Age Group	Living with Family Members	Living with Friends	Living Alone	Total
65 - 74	373 (86%)	37 (9%)	22 (5%)	432 (100%)
75 & above	145 (81%)	22 (12%)	13 (7%)	180 (100%)
Total	518 (85%)	59 (10%)	35 (5%)	612 (100%)

The social resources questionnaire examines social relationships with family and friends, availability of help when needed, loneliness and visits by relatives and friends. This is adapted from the Older American Resources and Services schedule (Duke OARS 1978). The overall rating of social resources is divided into 4 categories, i.e. good, mildly impaired, moderately impaired and severely impaired (Table 3.4). The majority of the elderly (78%) had good or mildly impaired social resources meaning that social relationships were satisfactory and at least one person would take care of him/her indefinitely or for a short term (Table 3.5). About 21% of young-old and 27% of old-old had moderate or severe impairment of social resources — their social relationships might or might not be satisfactory and help was available for a short term only or not at all.

Table 3.4: Social Resources Rating Scale
(Adapted from Duke OARS, 1978)

1. Good social resources
   Social relationships are satisfactory and at least one person would take care of him (her) indefinitely.

2. Mildly impaired
   Social relationships are unsatisfactory, but at least one person would take care of him (her) indefinitely.
   or
   Social relationships are satisfactory and only short term help is available.

3. Moderately impaired
   Social relationships are unsatisfactory and only short term care is available.
   or
   Social relationships are satisfactory; but help would only be available now and then.

4. Severely impaired
   Social relationships are unsatisfactory, and help would only be available now and then.
   or
   Social relationships are at least satisfactory or adequate; but help is not even available now and then.

It is alarming that over a quarter of the old-old had poor social resources, which would be vital in this age group because of declining health. In a recent study of elderly Malays in Singapore (Kua 1993 a) it appears that they have better social resources than the Chinese. About 99% of a sample of 149 elderly Malays in the Eunos district lived with their families and 1% with friends, 69% had good social resources, 28% mild impairment and only 3% moderate or severe impairment. All their married children lived in the vicinity and they also had good support from other relatives or neighbours.

Table 3.5: Social Resources

Age Group	Good	Mildly Impaired	Moderately Impaired	Severely Impaired	Total
65-74	272 (63%)	71 (16%)	58 (14%)	31 (7%)	432 (100%)
75 & above	109 (60%)	23 (13%)	23 (13%)	25 (14%)	180 (100%)
Total	381 (62%)	94 (16%)	81 (13%)	56 (9%)	612 (100%)

It is interesting to note that in this sample the main carer was not the children but the spouse. Because men tend to marry younger wives, elderly men usually have their wives to look after them, but elderly women are often widowed. In some cases where a couple was living together, it would be a frail elderly caring for another more frail spouse. An elderly woman confided that she was relieved when her husband eventually died of heart failure because she could not cope, for she was afflicted with severe arthritis herself. As most of the elderly in the sample were quite healthy, they did not require intense or constant care — they depended principally on their sons to provide for them or take them to see a doctor. However for those who needed more supervision it would be the womenfolk at home — daughters or daughters-in-law who provided the care. About 90% of the sample were certain of a family carer to look after them when they became infirm. However only 68% were quite definite of long-term care by the family. Long-term care is often necessary for those elderly with chronic illness, e.g. stroke.

The data emphasise that the family is the main provider for the elderly — they bear the brunt of health care. In order to encourage the family to continue this role, it is necessary to provide adequate community support services. This is especially urgent for those elderly with poor social resources. Supporting the family is important because sometimes elderly patients are referred to the hospital not because the illness has deteriorated but because the family could not cope anymore.

Table 3.6: Analysis of Social Support

1. Is there someone who would take care of you if you were sick or disabled.
   Yes   - 90%
   No   - 10%

2. If yes
Someone who would take care indefinitely	68%
Someone who would take care for a short while	16%
Someone who would help now and then	16%

3. Main carer or provider if unwell.
Spouse	48%
Daughter	14%
Son	24%
Daughter-in-law	2%
Others	2%
Nil	10%

4. Feeling of loneliness
Never	78%
Sometimes	18%
Yes	4%

A feeling of loneliness was elicited in 22% of the elderly interviewed but only 4% experienced this all the time. There was no relationship between loneliness and marital status or living arrangement, meaning that the frequency was not higher in singles, widowed or those living alone. This emphasises the distinction between loneliness and social isolation. An elderly who lives alone (socially isolated) may not feel lonely if he is able to interact with neighbours or friends — meet them occasionally or through telephone conversation. But an elderly living within the family may feel lonely if there is no interaction. Often this sense of loneliness could progress insidiously to depression. In old age friends may sometimes be valued more than relatives and friendship can be closer than kin relationship — there is often similarity in values, age, interest and dialect. In the three districts, old people often meet at the void decks of their flats, coffee shops, tea houses or community centres.

Friends are a source of emotional support and contributes to the elderly's sense of well being.

Leisure Activities

Young people often wonder, "Is there life after 65?" An elderly person once quipped, "Life begins after 65". After toiling for so many years, workers look forward to retirement as a time to reap the fruit of their labour. Preparation for retirement underscores the value of time management. There is no more the hustle of rushing to work, the routine of a tight daily schedule and exhaustion at the end of the day. Adjustment to retirement is usually more difficult for a working man than a housewife, who continues in her role at home. He loses the companionship of his colleagues and more importantly, the status of his job. The wife may not be accustomed to his presence in the house all the day and may even resent his intrusion into the kitchen. In fact, some elderly people would prefer to take up another job — full-time or part-time. It is said that the middle class adjust better in retirement because they have cultivated hobbies previously and retirement provides time for self actualisation. But working class people may have less time for hobbies and retirement does not confer financial security, necessitating re-employment.

Table 3.7 shows the leisure activities of the two age groups of elderly. Their favourite pastimes were watching television or listening to the radio, others included light exercises, visit to the community centres mainly to read the papers or meet friends. It means that the popular media to educate or inform elderly people would be through radio or television. As they were mainly from the working class, no one had taken on more expensive pursuits like golf or membership of private clubs. About a-fifth looked after grandchildren, allowing daughters or daughters-in-law to work outside the home, thus contributing indirectly to the national economy. It is unfortunate that only a minority had hobbies to help them enjoy their leisure. But many of them would congregate around the local coffee shop to listen to a bird-singing contest or watch a game of chess. Religious fervour is never quite intense among the Chinese in general unlike the Malays. Buddhism and Taoism are in fact philosophies which have been exalted to religious doctrines. Many elderly Chinese believe in Shenism — the worship of numerous deities who influence everyday living, i.e. wealth, health and death. This is different from the monotheism of Christianity and Islam. About 19% in the sample believed in Buddhism-Taoism, 65% Shenism, 1% Christianity and 15% had no religion. Only about one-fifth visited places of worship and the majority worshipped at home. Even those who visited the temples would do so infrequently and usually during festivals.

Table 3.7: Leisure Activities
(in percentage)

Activities	Age Group 65 - 74 (n = 432)	75 & more (n = 180)
Watch TV	79	73
Listen to radio	65	63
Walk or exercise	51	41
Read papers	50	13
Visit community centres	35	12
Visit friends	25	15
Look after grandchildren	21	14
Visit places of worship	19	10
Hobbies e.g. birds, fish, gardening	10	3

In the Ministry of Social Affairs nation wide survey of senior citizens (1983), the popular leisure activities were quite similar to the elderly in this sample (Table 3.8). In Japan it was reported that about 40% of the elderly were in cultural activities, 30% sports, 10% voluntarism and 7% educational programmes (JOICFP 1989). However the latter two activities are less popular amongst the Singapore elderly. Old people do have the potential to learn and educational courses have been found to be beneficial. In the United Kingdom, many elderly people enrol in the Open University or attend regularly short courses conducted by tertiary institutions on subjects as varied as history, law, literature, art, computer, etc. In this survey, only 0.5% of the sample, had been involved in voluntarism — they helped in elderly day centres, church or temple. In the United States and Europe, more elderly people volunteer their services in community work, like school, childcare, library, hospital, old people's home, etc. In the Singapore context where human resource is a scarce commodity, it may be possible to galvanise the healthy elderly to provide

Life after Sixty-Five

a volunteer service in caring for the frail elderly. This tradition was present when people lived together in small villages but less evident in high-rise housing estates.

It is surprising that only 2% of the elderly men frequented the 'clubs' run by their clan associations. When the early Chinese immigrants arrived in Singapore, those from the same province or dialect grouped together to form associations, or *huay kuan* which provided the social needs of the newcomers. They would go to these 'clubs' to exchange news about events in their village or debate about the politics of China. Today the clan associations are no longer the centripetal force which draws the various dialect groups together. The elderly Chinese women in the sample had a smaller social circle — they were never in the 'clubs' of the clan association and infrequently in community centre. Their friends were mainly the women folks of the neighbourhood and their social life revolved round the family.

Table 38: National Survey of Senior Citizens, Ministry of Social Affairs, 1983 (in percentage)

	Age Group	
	65-74 n = 1891	75 & more n = 765
Watch TV	90	80
Listen to radio	60	47
Walk or exercise	44	35
Visit places of worship	25	17
Visit friends	20	14

Working Elderly

The majority of subjects in the study were not working — 83% in the young-old and 93% in the old-old group (Table 3.9). However about 8% of the young-old and 1% of the old-old were still working full-time, as clerks, domestic servants, hawkers, shop-assistants, etc. Another 9% of the young-old and 6% of the old-old worked part-time. In the national survey of senior citizen (Ministry of Social Affairs 1983), it was found that 23% of the young-old and 12% of the old-old were still in employment (full or part-time). The discrepancy is because many of the working elderly were not included in the survey because they were not at home and could not be interviewed. In Japan, 50% of elderly men and 17% of elderly woman are employed. It is untrue that all elderly people are not productive. Many in the sample had to work to eke out a living because they had no pension, Central Provident Fund or insurance. They had laboured in an era of low wages with no union or representation to champion their cause. Some of them continued to work because, as one lamented, "I've nothing else to do — it helps to pass the time." For them, work was the only panacea to prevent ennui.

Table 3.9: Occupational Status

Age Group	Working Full-time	Working Part-time	Not Working	Total
65 - 74	33 (8%)	39 (9%)	360 (83%)	432 (100%)
75 & above	2 (1%)	11 (6%)	167 (93%)	180 (100%)
Total	35 (6%)	50 (8%)	527 (86%)	612 (100%)

Work confirms a role and status in the community. It has been observed that in a rural community, the elderly continue to maintain a role, probably in performing less exacting tasks in the farm or plantation, and they also assume a venerable position in the extended family. However in the urban setting there is less opportunity for gradual transitional change, and elderly people may become uncertain about their role in the community or family. In a society where the dominant value is productivity, elderly people become stigmatised as takers and not givers. This would inadvertently influenced young people's perception of the elderly.

Dependence and Independence

One of the worries in late life is the fear of ill health and becoming dependent on others. Sometimes it is this dependence that plagues the elderly more than the pain of the illness. There is no doubt that all elderly people prefer to make their own choices and to do their own things. But often because of illness, movement is restricted and activities limited.

Life after Sixty-Five

With the dwindling number of carers at home, it may just be the spouse (usually the wife) who becomes the sole care provider. In other circumstances it may be a daughter or daughter-in-law. But not uncommonly, no family member or friend is available. Some illnesses like stroke or dementia may linger on for 5 to 10 years and the demand on the carers is exacting.

The questionnaire in the survey explored the elderly person's degree of independence in activities of daily living, i.e. walking, feeding, bathing, toiletting, dressing, light chores (cleaning, washing, sweeping), shopping and looking. These activities are to a large extent a measure of independent living and their performance could be assessed as a rating scale (Table 3.10).

Table 3.10:
Performance Rating Scale for Activities of Daily Living
(Adapted from OARS, 1978)

1.	***Good ADL capacity*** Can perform all the Activities of Daily Living without assistance.
2.	***Mildly impaired ADL capacity*** Can perform all but one to three of the Activities of Daily Living. Some help is required, but not necessarily everyday. Can get through any single day without help.
3.	***Moderately impaired ADL capacity*** Regularly requires assistance with at least four Activities of Daily Living. Needs help each day but not necessarily throughout the day or night.
4.	***Severely impaired ADL capacity*** Needs help throughout the day and/or night to carry out the Activities of Daily Living.

Comparing the two age groups, 2.5% of the young-old and 15% of the old-old were moderately or severely impaired and needed help every day (Table 3.11). About 53% of the old-old and 67% of the young-old could perform all the activities of the daily living without assistance, and 32% of the old-old and 30.5% of the young-old required some assistance. The difference in the performance rating of the two groups is very significant, showing that the old-old were less independent. In the United Kingdom, the general Household Surveys (Victor 1987) reported comparable results: good ADL in 59% of women and 72% of men aged between 65-69, and 47% of women and 60% of men aged 70-79; these proportions decreasing with the aged 75-79, and 17% of women and 34% men aged 80 and more.

Table 3.11: Activities of Daily Living

Age Group	Good	Mildly Impaired	Moderately Impaired	Severely Impaired	Total
65 - 74	289 (67%)	132 (30.5%)	9 (2%)	2 (0.5%)	432 (100%)
75 & above	96 (53%)	58 (32%)	18 (10.5%)	8 (4.5%)	180 (100%)
Total	385 (63%)	190 (31%)	27 (4%)	10 (2%)	612 (100%)

The survey indicates that the majority of elderly people in Singapore could cope on their own. Combining the 'mildly-impaired' with the 'good' groups, 94% of the sample were independent and could manage with the necessary activities of daily living. This will be a revelation for those who wrongly surmise that elderly people are frail and need care daily. A common myth is that all elderly people need some care and cannot live independently. In fact only 6% of the sample had difficulties in carrying out the essential tasks of daily living. They are dependent on the family and made demands on the health services.

4

THE MIND IN OLD AGE

The cognitive changes in late life are sometimes imperceptible and vary with every individual. Intellect and memory may remain intact in the octogenarian. The deterioration is subtle and elderly people do compensate for the deficit. For example, a person with benign or normal forgetfulness of senescence may use a diary to help him remember the inventory for marketing. The intellectual deterioration of a scholar is more difficult to detect in the early phase of decline. Is there indeed a decline in intelligence with age? The concept of intelligence is sometimes vague and amorphous — it has been operationalised in a variety of ways using different psychological tests to measure different abilities. In general, intelligence refers to ability to think, solve problems and learn new task. There is no direct measure of intelligence and the tests involve a range of tasks, which assess verbal or performance skills.

    Elderly people generally perform poorly on intelligence tests because of time limitation on tests, sensory defects, easy fatigability and distractability. They are sometimes uncooperative because they perceive the tests as trivial and fear doing badly. Therefore test material and administration procedure must be appropriate for the elderly. Verbal skill involves language and words, and tends to decline less with age. Performances skill concerns visual and spatial aptitude which shows more decline with age. Elderly people may not think or act faster than young people and may have more difficulties in adjustment to a new job or unfamiliar situation. However for familiar tasks, they can draw on their experience to develop more efficient ways of doing a job.

    Older adults may also possess specialised knowledge and abilities not easily assessed by intelligence tests, but which may enable them to be more competent than young adults. Creative abilities of many people may continue till the seventh or eighth decades of life. Musicians like Horowitz and Rubinstein, and painters like Rembrandt and Picasso, have proven that creative productivity improves with years — in fact this 'crystallised intelligence' based on accumulated learning, tends to persist.

When is forgetfulness pathological or abnormal? In general, there are three processes in learning and remembering: firstly acquisition, secondly storage and then recall. The various stages can be disrupted by numerous factors, e.g. a depressed elderly may have a problem in concentration and hence the acquisition phase is affected. A patient with a brain pathology like Alzheimer's disease will have problems in all the stages. The traditional classification of types of memory are immediate, short-term and long-term memory. Immediate memory is only for a few minutes. Short-term memory has to do with remembering things more than 15 minutes to a few weeks. Long-term memory is recall of events in the distant past, e.g. childhood experiences.

In the survey, all the subjects were assessed for any difficulty with memory, what they would tend to forget (names of family members or friends) and also a 15-minute test recall of a four-digit number. Analysis of the results is shown in Table 4.1. About 65% of the sample said that they had become more forgetful especially with names and dates but only 4% had difficulty in the 15-minute recall. The majority of this latter group were suffering from dementia or depressive disorder. In normal ageing or senescence, immediate and long-term memories are usually intact. Subtle changes occur with short-term memory, e.g. forgetting the house keys or the shopping list but there is no steady or accelerate decline. But in abnormal or pathological forgetfulness of dementia, the change is gross, e.g. the person cannot remember having been to see the doctor that morning, although events which occur 10 years ago may still be recalled. It must be emphasised that in old age, forgetfulness does not necessarily imply dementia.

Table 4.1: Memory Assessment of Sample (n=612)

Complaint of forgetfulness	Yes	65%
	No	35%
15-minute recall test	Poor	4%
	Good	96%

Changes in sleeping habit are not uncommon in old age. The disturbance may be due to the physiological process of normal ageing or due to sleep disorders. The circadian sleep-wake rhythm in elderly people can mean an increased night time wakefulness and day time fatigue. Elderly people are more easily aroused from sleep by environmental stimuli, like noise or light. Electrical recording of the brain waves of normal elderly people during sleep by the electroencephalogram or EEG, shows more light sleep and less deep sleep. Sleep problems in old age are often due to pain (e.g. arthritis, angina, etc.), breathing discomfort (e.g. asthma, bronchitis, heart failure, etc.) or psychiatric illness (e.g. depression and anxiety). In the survey, 25% of the subjects had sleep problems — 16% associated with physical ill health and 9% with psychiatric illness. The main complaints were difficulty falling asleep and frequent awakening (Table 4.2). A compliant of insomnia does not necessarily mean that the person needs a hypnotic or sleeping pill. Insomnia or inability to sleep, is merely a symptom. In this studies about 3% of the elderly were prescribed hypnotics, mainly the benzodiazepines like diazepam.

Table 4.2: Sleeping Behaviour of Sample (n=612)

Any trouble with asleep	Yes	25%
	No	75%
Difficulty falling asleep	-	18%
Frequent awakening	-	12%
Early morning awakening	-	2%

*Some subjects had more than one symptom of sleep disorder.

Mental State Assessment

The interview instrument for mental health assessment in the survey was derived from the pioneering work of Copeland *et al.* (1976) and Gurland *et al.* (1976), who together constructed a semi-structured clinical interview schedule called the Geriatric Mental State or GMS. This instrument has been shown to be reliable between trained interviewers and it can also provide a standardised psychiatric diagnosis with the computerised system, Automated Geriatric Examination for Computer

Assisted Taxonomy (AGECAT). Concordance between psychiatrists and AGECAT in making diagnoses has been shown to be high (Copeland *et al.* 1986). For use in the community a shortened version of the GMS called GMSA has been developed. In general, it takes about 30-45 minutes to administer the GMS.

In the Singapore context, certain questions in the GMS need modification because of cultural differences. For example, many Chinese elderly remember their date of birth according to the Chinese calendar and tend to add one more year to their age. According to Chinese custom a baby is one year old at birth. Therefore the question on the difference in birth date and age, has to take into consideration the subject's overestimation by a year. Similarly in the assessment of orientation, very often the elderly give the Chinese date, and a knowledge of the Chinese calendar is important to check their answers.

All the subjects with suspected mental disorders were further investigated. The laboratory tests were to exclude conditions which could mimic depressive disorder or dementia. Some of these include brain tumour, thyroid disorder, nutritional deficiencies, head injury, syphilis, kidney disease and liver disease. The investigations included a full blood count, blood urea and electrolytes, thyroid function test, VDRL, chest x-ray and if indicated, computerised tomography of the brain.

The criteria of diagnosis in this study are based on the International Classification of Diseases, Ninth Revision (World Health Organization 1978).

Dementia

This is the most dreaded disease in late life. It is a syndrome in which there is impairment of orientation in time, place or person, poor short-term memory, comprehension, learning capacity and judgement. These are the classical features but there may also be liability of mood, lowering of ethical standards and exaggeration of personality traits, and eventually a diminished capacity for independent living. The two common types of dementia are:

a. ***Alzheimer's Disease*** or Senile Dementia, which occurs usually after the age of 65, is a progressive disease of insidious onset. Symptoms of Alzheimer's disease include a gradual memory loss, decline in ability to perform routine tasks, disorientation in time and space, impairment of judgement, personality change, difficulty in learning, and loss of language and communication skills. From the onset of symptoms, the life span of an Alzheimer victim can range anywhere from 3 to 20 or more years. The disease eventually leaves its victims unable to care for themselves.

b. ***Multi-infarct Dementia (MID)*** is attributable to degenerative arterial disease of the brain. Symptoms suggest a focal lesion in the brain. There is a deterioration of mental capabilities caused by multiple strokes (infarcts) in the brain. The onset of MID may be relatively sudden as many strokes can occur before symptoms appear. These strokes may damage areas of the brain to produce generalised symptoms of dementia.

Studies on dementia in many countries show wide variation in the prevalence rate (Table 4.3). In mild dementia, Parsons in Wales (1965) reported a high rate of 21.9% compared with 1.5% by Hasegawa in Japan (1974). There are more consistent findings in severe dementia and the range is between 5.6% (Kay *et al.* 1964a) and 0.7% (Shibayama 1986). Some reasons for the variation include differences in interview instruments and diagnostic criteria.

Table 4.3: Surveys of Dementia in the Community

Author	Country	Prevalence(%) Mild	Severe
Kay *et al.* (1964 a)	England	5.7	5.6
Parsons (1965)	Wales	21.9	4.4
Hasegawa (1974)	Japan	1.5	1.6
Gurland *et al.* (1983)	USA	-	4.9
	England	-	2.3
Shibayama *et al.* (1986)	Japan	-	0.7
Copeland *et al.* (1987)	England	-	5.2

In the survey there were 11 cases of dementia, 5 in the young-old and 6 in the old-old. The prevalence of dementia in the young-old was 1.1% and this increased to 3.3% in the old-old. There were 7 with dementia of the Alzheimer's type and for multi-infarct dementia, there were 3 cases in the young-old and one in the old-old. The prevalence of Alzheimer's disease was 1.1% and multi-infarct dementia 0.7%. There were 5 women and 2 men with Alzheimer's disease, and 2 women and men with multi-infarct dementia. Comparing the sex distribution, the prevalence of Alzheimer's diseases was higher in women (1.5%) than in men (0.6%). In multi-infarct dementia, the prevalence rate was similar at 0.7% (Table 4.4). When the data from the interview were keyed into the computer program, AGECAT, there were 14 cases of dementia diagnosed, and hence a prevalence of 2.3% — the concordance between computer and psychiatrist's diagnosis achieved kappa value of 0.87.

Table 4.4: Prevalence of Dementia (in percentage)

Type of Dementia	Men	Women
Alzheimer's Disease	0.7	1.5
Multi-infarct Dementia	0.7	0.6

Caring for demented patients depends also on how independent they are. Three cases of dementia in the young-old had mild impairment in activities of daily living (ADL) and two had moderate impaired ADL which means daily care and supervision are necessary. In the old-old, all the six cases were moderately impaired. Eight cases had good social resources, meaning that they were well supported by their families and care would be available indefinitely. Two cases had mild impairment of social resources — their social relationship was satisfactory but their children felt that they could not continue to take care of them for a long time. Only one elderly had moderate impairment of social resources — she was single and shared a flat with another friend. Her social relationship was satisfactory but help would only be available now and then. Arrangement had been made by a hospital social worker to transfer her to an institutional home.

All the family carers expressed feelings of social isolation, but none of them would like to send their elderly parents to an institutional home. They felt embarrassed, ashamed and guilty about abdicating their duty. A few had employed domestic help to assist. In the main, all of them had little or no information about dementia and did not know how to take care of those who were restless — these cases were usually locked inside rooms or tied to chairs or beds. They felt ashamed of the unpredictable behaviour of their demented parents and even advised their children not to invite friends homes. The family carers were either daughters or daughters-in-law. Two of the carers had to resign from full-time jobs and another could only work part-time.

In an international review of the epidemiology of dementia, Henderson (1988) wrote that an important factor contributing to variation in prevalence of dementia in many studies was the age structure of the population surveyed. With increasing age there is an increased tendency to develop dementia. There is a remarkable increase in the prevalence, amounting to a four to seven-fold change from 70-79 to ages greater than 80 (Mortimer *et al.* 1981). It is estimated that the prevalence rate of dementia for different ages rise gradually from 2% in the age group 65 to 69 to 5% in those 75-79 years and 22% in those above 80 years. In the meta-analysis of 22 different studies, Jorm *et al.* (1987) found that the prevalence doubled every 5.1 years up to the age of 95.

Recent surveys on the epidemiology of dementia in elderly people living in the community, using the GMS schedule, were conducted in the cities of New York, London, Hobart, Liverpool and Beijing. In the cross-national study of elderly people in New York and London, Gurland *et al.* (1983) used the CARE interview schedule developed from the GMS. All subjects in the London sample were interviewed by psychiatrists but in New York, only half the sample were interviewed by psychiatrists and the rest by social scientists who were trained in the interview method. In the London study, a random sample of elderly subjects was drawn from the general practitioners' register and in New York the sample was drawn from the State Office for Ageing. The prevalence rate of dementia in New York was estimated as 4.9% and London 2.3% — both cities had higher rates than Singapore.

Using the GMS (Canberra version), Kay *et al.* (1985) surveyed 274 elderly living in Hobart. For those between 70-79 years the prevalence of mild dementia was 3.8% and moderate dementia 2.5%. Those 80 years and above had a rate of 17.2% for mild dementia and 7.8% for moderate or severe dementia. In a recent study of 1070 elderly persons living in the Liverpool community, Copeland *et al.* (1987) used the GMS shortened version and the findings were processed to provide a computerised diagnosis by AGECAT. The prevalence of dementia was calculated at 5.2%, with women 6.8% and men 2.7%. The Beijing study was conducted in 1986 and included 1,090 subjects aged 60 years and above (Li *et al.* 1989). The survey was conducted in two stages — first screening using the Mini Mental State Examination (Folstein *et al.* 1975). Suspected cases were examined with the GMS. Calculating the prevalence of dementia for those 65 years or more shows a remarkable similarity to the Singapore study of 1.8 %. In Beijing, the prevalence of Alzheimer's disease was 0.6% — this is lower than Singapore (1.1%).But for multi-infarct dementia, Beijing had a higher prevalence of 1.1% compared to Singapore 0.7%.

Sex difference in the two types of dementia has indicated a preponderance of women with senile dementia or Alzheimer's disease and men with multi-infarct dementia (Roth 1978). However the Scandinavian studies by Persson (1980) found a higher proportion of men with senile dementia. The Singapore study showed a higher prevalence of Alzheimer's disease in women but no sex difference for multi-infarct dementia. In a study of elderly Malays in Singapore (Kua 1993 c) it was found that for men the rate of Alzheimer's disease and multi-infarct dementia were similar at 1.2%; but for women the rate of Alzheimer's disease was 1.5% and multi-infarct dementia 4.4%.

Epidemiological research is valuable to provide data for future planning of health and social services. Without the basic data it will be difficult to plan for the appropriate levels and types of services required. Knowing the prevalence of dementia in elderly people in Singapore, it is possible to estimate the number of cases in the total population in the near future. As shown in Table 4.5 the number of cases of dementia will increase from 2,550 in 1985 to about 4,100 in 2000. The rise will be phenomenal after this as the number increases to 12,400 in 2030. The data have to be interpreted for the Chinese population only.

Depressive Disorder

The most common psychiatric illness of old age is depressive disorder (Henderson and Kay 1984). Psychiatric referrals in a general hospital also indicated a higher proportion of depression than other disorders (Kua 1987 a). There is a distinction between being depressed and depressive disorder. Those who suffer from depressive disorder are depressed but not everyone who is depressed has depressive disorder. The symptoms of depressive disorder are low mood, insomnia, a loss of interest, lethargy, poor appetite, weight loss, tearfulness, pessimism, indecision, poor concentration and somatic symptoms of headache, tension or chest discomfort. There is often preoccupation with the psychic trauma which precedes the illness, e.g. loss of a cherished person or possession.

Table 4.5: Estimated Number of Dementia in Singapore 1985-2030

Age	Prevalence	1985	2000	2030
65 - 74	1.1%	1,050	1,500	4,400
75 & above	3.3%	1,500	2,600	8,000
Total	1.8%	2,550	4,1001	2,400

In the survey there were 28 elderly with depressive disorder — 23 in the young-old and 5 in the old-old (Table 4.5). There were 10 men and 18 women, and the prevalence rate for women (5.4%) was one and a half times higher than men (3.6%). About 64% of the depressed group were in social class IV and V compared with 69% of non-depressed elderly — the difference is not statistically significant. About 53% of the depressed elderly were widowed compared with 46% of non-depressed elderly, and the difference is also not significant. Seventeen of the depressed group (60%) had good social resources, meaning that their social relationships were satisfactory and there would be a relative to take care of them indefinitely or for a short term. A significant finding was that 39% more of the depressed group had moderate or severe impairment of social resource compared with only 21% of non-depressed elderly.

Analysis of the data by the AGECAT computer showed that there were 35 cases of depressive disorder and a prevalence of 5.7%. The concordance between the computer and psychiatrist had a kappa value of 0.88, which is very acceptable in research.

Table 4.5: Age Distribution of Depressive Disorder

Age Group	Number of Persons at Risk	Number of Cases	Prevalence (%)
65 - 74	432	23	5.3
75 & above	180	5	2.7
Total	612	28	4.6

The social origin of depression in late life has been explored by many research workers. A survey in Australia showed that depressed elderly had markedly less social interaction than the mentally normal elderly (Henderson et al. 1986). Murphy (1986) noted that elderly people without a confidant were more vulnerable to depression. Kay et al. (1964b) observed that complaint of loneliness and not social isolation, was associated with depression. A study in Finland (Pahkala 1990) found that low social participation was associated with depression in elderly women. Blazer (1980) reported the inverse relationship between the prevalence of depressive disorder and social class. The author suggested that the relationship was indirect because the lower social class had a higher rate of social difficulties (e.g. bad housing) and poor physical health.

The majority of the depressed subjects in this study had good or mild impairment of performance in activities of daily living. Only 18% of the depressed group compared with 4% of the mentally normal elderly had moderate or severe impairment — this difference is very significant ($p < 0.001$). The physical health of majority of depressed subjects was good or mildly impaired — 10 with mild impairment had complaints of arthritis, poor vision, partial deafness, diabetes mellitus or hypertension. Six with moderate or severe impairment had ischaemic heart disease, stroke, cancer and renal failure. Poor physical health affects activities of daily living and invariably limits independent living. The elderly may be upset or worried by their dependence on others and especially if there is conflict with the carer at home. Physical illness, e.g. ischaemic heart disease, cancer, stroke and renal failure, could also lead to depression. Post (1969) had commented on the association between depression and physical illness like stroke and poor vision or hearing, which would cause a loss of independence, morale and hope.

The subjects were also asked about their principal worry and the responses are shown in Table 4.6. The commonest worry of the depressed group concerned family relationships (50%) — the conflicts were usually with children or children-in-law. These problems were often long-standing and might have been aggravated by the elderly being forced by circumstances to live together with the children. For example, a widower was unable to manage alone after the death of his wife and had to live with his son and daughter-in-law whom he had never got on well in the past. Because of the strained relationship, many elderly worried about whether their children would be willing to take care of them in later years or whether they would be sent to an institutional home. Only 8% of the non-depressed elderly had problem of family conflict — the main worry of this group was personal health (16%). About a fifth of the depressed group also cited personal health as a source of grave concern. Five depressed elderly spoke about financial problems; they were not receiving public assistance and were dependent on their children for allowances. There were 3 depressed elderly who had to look after sick relatives. One widow was caring for a mentally retarded daughter, and two women were looking after their husbands who were severely ill. All of them had poor social support — the widow had no other relatives, one couple had no children and another couple had three married children who seldom visited them.

Studies of depression in the elderly in different cultures provide different statistical data. In the New York-London survey on the mental health of the elderly, Gurland *et al.* (1983) reported a prevalence of 13% for New York and 12.4% London. There was a decrease in prevalence rate from 65 to 79 years in both cities, but in New York the rate increased after 80 years while in London it remained steady. The rate for women was higher in both cities but after 80 the rate for men in New York exceeded that of women. Kay *et al.* (1985) studied depression in elderly people living in the Hobart community and found the prevalence in the 70 to

79 years to be 12.7% for mild depression and 13.9% for moderate and severe depression; and in those 80 years and more, 20.9% for mild depression and 14.8% for moderate and severe depression.

Table 4.6: Types of Worries
(in percentage)

Worries	Depressed Elderly (n=28)	Non-depressed Elderly (n=584)
Family relationship	50	8
Personal health	21	16
Finance	18	10
Relative's health	11	4
None	-	62
Total	100%	100%

The higher prevalence in New York, London and Hobart compared to Singapore cannot merely be due to differences in methodology and diagnostic criteria. In all the four cities, the GMS schedule or modified version of the GMS were used. A possible factor for the difference in rates is the socio-cultural influence on perception of elderly people in Chinese society. The emphasis on respect for the elderly, filial piety and family support for elderly parents may be crucial in minimising stress in old age. Confucian ethics which permeate into family life, underscore the importance of the family in caring for the elderly. Families prefer to care for their elderly rather than to send them to an institution. More of the elderly subjects in New York, London and Hobart compared to Singapore were living alone.

The common symptoms of depressive disorder in this study were a feeling of sadness, insomnia, headache, tension and pessimism. The association between somatic symptoms and depressive disorder has been well documented by Wilson *et al.* (1982) and Katon (1984). These authors noted that depressed patients in primary care clinics often presented with

Keeping fit

Staying busy........

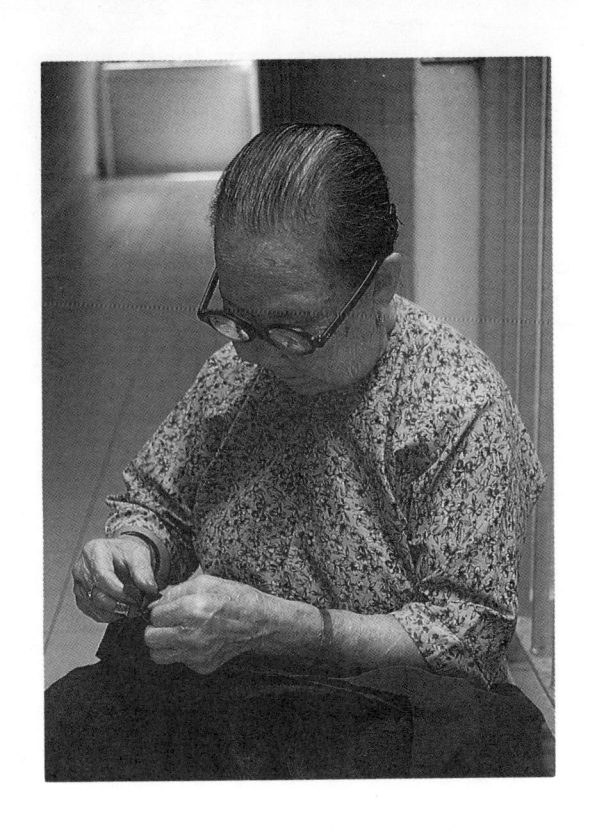

.......and occupied

Relaxing.......

pain as a complaint, such as abdominal pain, chronic headache and low back pain. The high frequency of somatisation in depressed Chinese had been reported by Tseng (1975). In a study of 100 patients suffering from 'neurasthenia' in an outpatient clinic at Hunan, China, Kleinman (1982) noted that 87 had major depression; all presented with somatic symptoms, especially headache. It was suggested by Yap (1965) that poorly educated people with depression tended to somatise more often. In the Singapore sample 57% of the depressed elderly had headache, 25% chest discomfort, 50% feelings of tension and 36% lethargy.

Four of the elderly with depressive disorder had suicidal tendency but had never planned or acted on this thought. Two of them had been debilitated by coronary heart disease and stroke; and spoke about wishing to end their lives to alleviate the pain and burden on the family. The other two were tearful when they talked about their children who neglected them — they had also mild disabilities from arthrities. A salient finding of suicide studies in many countries is the consistently high rate for elderly people (Lindesay 1986; Blazer *et al.* 1986; McClure 1987). Although suicide as a cause of death in the elderly is insignificant compared with cancer or coronary heart disease, a significant fact is that suicide is preventable. In Singapore there may be an underestimation of the number of suicides because of the strict legal definition of the term suicide. A verdict of suicide is recorded by the Coroner if these is clear evidence that the injury was self-inflicted and the deceased intended to kill himself. If there is any doubt about intent, then an accidental or open verdict is recorded.

In a study of suicide in Singapore from 1985-88 (Kua & Ko 1992), it was found that the mean annual suicide rate for the general population was 12 per 100,000 but in the elderly population the rate was highest in the Chinese (61 per 100,000), followed by Indians (30 per 100,000) and Malays (3 per 100,000). The low Malay suicide rate in Singapore and Malaysia has been documented (Kua & Tsoi 1985, Teoh 1974). Their strong Islamic belief and less competitive life style have been cited as possible reasons for the abhorrence of suicidal behaviour. Comparing elderly male and female suicide in the Chinese, the rate was higher in men (68 per 100,000) than women (48 per 100,000), elderly Indian women had also a lower rate (25 per 100,000) than men (36 per 100,000). There was no apparent sex difference for the Malays (Table 4.6). The mean suicide rate was the highest in Chinese men. This is similar to studies in the United States (Miller 1978) and Britain (McClure 1987) where reports indicated a male preponderance in elderly suicide. Many elderly people today do not have any pension or adequate savings. They are therefore dependent on their children for financial assistance. But for the elderly who are unmarried, the situation can be quite dismal—especially when they live alone and are frail. The common methods of suicide by elderly people were jumping from high-rise buildings (61%) and hanging (31%). Other less common methods were self-poisoning with pesticide or weedicide (4%), drowning (2%) and others (2%)—death from firearm was uncommon.

Table 4.7: Mean Annual Suicide rate in Singapore, 1985-88
(rate per 100,000 population)

Age Groups	Chinese Male	Chinese Female	Indians Male	Indians Female	Malays Male	Malays Female
10 - 64 years	15	10	12	4	6	3
65 years and more	68	48	36	25	3	3

The studies by Sainbury (1955) and Barraclough (1971) had underlined the association between depression and suicide. The high incidence of physical illness in elderly suicide had also been reported by Barraclough (1971) and Whitlock (1978). The sociological theory of suicide in the elderly supports Durkheim's concept of anomie (1951). Suicide may result from social isolation due to a breakdown of social bond. This may be due to death of a spouse, separation or children leaving home. Elderly people who live alone or isolate themselves are especially susceptible to depression because of the absence of a confiding relationship (Murphy 1982). In Singapore it had been noted that many of the elderly suicides were male Chinese immigrants who were unmarried and unskilled labourers, who were poor and lived alone (Chia 1981).

What happened to the 28 depressed elderly after 5 years? On follow up it was found that 8 (29%) recovered, 5 (18%) died, 2 (7%) had anxiety disorder and 9 (32%) were still depressed; the remaining 4 were untraceable (Kua 1993 b). The outcome was rather gloomy and the follow-up study in Liverpool (Copeland *et al.* 1992) also reflected a poor result. Only two depressed elderly had antidepressant treatment. Most of the elderly Chinese in the study tended to consult traditional healers, who had 'clinics' on the ground floor of the flats. The traditional healers or 'sinseh' are popular with the elderly not only because of the accessibility of their service but also because they share the same socio-cultural belief about illness and health.

Anxiety Disorder

This condition manifests as various combinations of physical and mental symptoms of anxiety, not attributable to real danger and occurring either in attacks or as a persisting state. The common symptoms of anxiety disorder are palpitation, sweating, giddiness, tightness of chest, numbness of hands, weakness, tension and insomnia.

In this study there were six cases of anxiety disorder — five in the young-old group and one in the old-old. The prevalence was 1.2% in the young-old and 0.6% in the old-old. Of the six cases, there were five women and one man. The common symptoms of anxiety disorder experienced by the six cases were a feeling of tension, mild headache, palpitation and difficulty in asleep. The two cases of recurrent anxiety disorder also complained of difficulty in relaxing and brief episodes of depression. On the social resources rating scale all had good social support, meaning that there was someone who would take care of them indefinitely and social relationships with family or friends were satisfactory. Assessment of physical health showed that two were in good physical health and four had mild impairment like arthritis, diabetes mellitus and hypertension. All were mobile and needed no assistance in walking. The survey in Liverpool by Copeland *et al.* (1987) showed a prevalence of 2.4% for anxiety disorder, and the rate for women was 3.5% and men 0.7%.

Paranoid Disorder

This is an uncommon mental disorder in late life and has the principal symptom of delusion especially of being influenced, persecuted or treated in some special way. There were only three cases of paranoid disorder in this study — two women and one man — giving a prevalence of 0.5%. All were married, retired and lived with their families. On physical examination, two were in good health and one was partially deaf. The three cases fit the concept of late paraphrenia which is defined as 'a well organised system of paranoid delusions with or without auditory, hallucinations existing in the setting of well preserved personality'. Grahame (1984) studied 25 patients and found that 14 had auditory hallucinations and delusions. The association between hearing difficulty and paranoid disorder had been reported by Post (1966). Paranoid disorder in late life are uncommon and most cases are in mental hospitals. In the Liverpool community survey of the elderly Copeland *et al.* (1987) estimated the prevalence as 1.0%.

Although paranoid disorder is uncommon it is the commonest diagnosis of elderly patients admitted to the mental hospital at Woodbridge (Kua *et al.* 1983). Many were admitted because of the disturbance they created when for example they encountered their 'persecutors'. They often settled quickly after admission to hospital and the majority were dischanged within 6 months of admission. These patients have to continue anti-psychotic medication for many years.

Psychogeriatric Service

Caring for elderly people with dementia at home is exacting and distressing (Green and Timburg 1979, Gray and Isaacs, Gilleard *et al.* 1982, Gilleard 1984). The emotional and social burden on families can be devastating (Koin 1989). They have to adjust or cope with loss of employment and social isolation (Anderson 1987). Carers need to seek help outside the home. Community and governmental supports are necessary to alleviate the burden of care. Presently in Singapore psychogeriatric service is not very satisfactory (Ministry of Community Development 1988). Day care facilities cater only for those elderly with physical illness like stroke. A day centre for dementia has now been established but there is no provision for the depressed elderly. Most homes are reluctant to accept the demented because they cannot cope with them. A lack of planning of services to meet the needs of the demented elderly can lead to serious consequences when the number of cases exceeds 12,000 in the year 2030.

The angst about caring for an increasing number of demented elderly had been observed in the west (Mortimer *et al.* 1981, Arie and Jolley 1983, Mahendra 1985, Katzman 1986). The organisation of a comprehensive psycho-geriatric service had been discussed by Arie and Jolley (1982). The essential facilities in a psychogeriatric service should include a day care centre, hospital beds (a ward either in a mental or general hospital) and respite care. The day care centre provides facilities for assessment and management. Moreover, the day care service also permits early discharge of hospitalised patients and continuity of care. Because the patients could come during the day and return home in the evening, this allows carers to work and provide succour or relief in the day time. Occasionally due to behavioural disturbance, it may be necessary to admit the patient to a hospital. In certain circumstances, such as when the carer is unwell or wants to go for a holiday, the patient can be admitted for a short period into a respite care service.

Patients with mild dementia but no behavioural problems can be managed in their own homes. They are ambulant and carers can usually cope. Sometimes they may require day care for continuing management and rehabilitation. Day care and hospitalisation are more often utilised by cases with moderate and severe dementia. The official recommendations of the Department of Health and Social Security in the United Kingdom for severe dementia are 2 to 3 hospital beds and 2 day care places per 1000 elderly population.

It will be impossible provide a psychogeriatric service if there are insufficient mental health professionals. The multidisciplinary team includes the psychogeriatrician, nurses, social workers, occupational therapists and psychologists. Providing training, local and overseas, for health professional in psychogeriatrics should be encouraged. Because mental illness is often associated with physical illness in late life, many patients may need to consult a geriatrician, who will play an important role in the team. Community-based services should also include the general practitioners who are often the first health professionals to make contact with the elderly person. Because undergraduate medical training in geriatric medicine or psychiatry is minimal, very often early cases of dementia are not recognised by the general practitioners. To improve early detection, a simple 10-item questionnaire (Elderly Cognitive Assessment Questionnaire or ECAQ) to screen for cognitive impairment has been developed by the author specially for elderly people in developing countries (Appendix 1).

The principal aim in the provision of psychiatric service for the elderly should be to prevent the occurrence of handicap whenever possible and to remedy it as far as possible. Primary prevention for depression could begin with the keeping of a register of those elderly who are prone to develop the disorder. The high risk group includes those with a past history of depressive disorder, poor social support and physical disabilities that needed care. Of utmost importance in primary prevention would be to encourage elderly people to remain active mentally and physically, and to avoid social withdrawal. The emphasis on filial piety and respect for the elderly in young people will help to improve family relationships. Public education programmes have been organised to promote intergenerational relationships, strengthen traditional family ties and interaction between grandparents, parents and children. These programmes through the mass media promote understanding of the social and psychological aspects of ageing, foster positive attitudes towards the elderly and emphasise family care.

   Secondary prevention means the early diagnosis and treatment of depressive disorder. Doctors in the primary care team can refer cases to a psychogeriatric assessment unit, which could be situated in a day care centre. A few depressed elderly may require inpatient treatment and they are usually those who are suicidal or psychotic. However, the majority of cases can be treated as outpatients. Finally, tertiary prevention is to prevent institutional neurosis or further deterioration of mental health. A day care service allows early discharge of hospitalised patients, who can continue treatment in the day care centre, where there are usually a range of therapies, e.g. occupational therapy, physiotherapy, group therapy and social therapy.

5
PHYSICAL HEALTH

One of the preoccupations of elderly people is health. As mentioned previously, the majority in the sample surmised that a deterioration of their health heralded the onset of ageing. However it is a rueful myth that ageing is synonymous with infirmity and debility. This has portentous repercussion — young people would perceive elderly parents as a burden, a liability or an impediment to their career (if they are carers). Such stereotypes are pervasive and sometimes perpetuated by the popular press and television where the elderly are protrayed as frail and disabled, in dire need of care, shuffling aimlessly and muttering incoherently along the lonely corridors of old folks' home. Such images are imprinted in the memory, and subconsciously, 'ageism' crystallises. Employers think that the over 55 workers are sickly and need to retire. People dread retirement and are even reluctant to disclose their age. It is true that elderly people in general tend to consult doctors more often than young people. But sometimes they dismiss their symptoms as due to old age and even doctors collude with this myth and tend to ignore them. It is assumed that aches and pains are an integral part of ageing and elderly people should be stoic and not complain!

A physical examination was conducted for all the subjects in the survey. The nurse informed them of this free service to encourage them to participate. Those who could not come to the day centres because of ill health were examined at home. The physical health rating is from a scale of 1 to 4 corresponding to good physical health, mild, moderate and severe physical impairment (Table 5.1). The classification depends on whether the illness or disability is painful, life threatening and needs extensive medical treatment. This rating is adapted from the Older American Resources and Services (Duke OARS 1978).

The physical health of the elderly in the sample is seen in Table 5.2. In the young-old group, 54% were in good physical health and 43% had minor disabilities. In the old-old, 49% were in good health and 38% had minor disabilities. About 3% of young-old and 13% of old-old had moderate or severe impairment of physical health. Comparing the two age groups, the physical health of the old-old was more impaired ($p < 0.001$).

Table 5.1: Physical Health Rating Scale

1. ***In good physical health***
   No significant illness or disabilities.

2. ***Mildly impaired***
   Has only minor illnesses and/or disabilities which might benefit from medical treatment or corrective measures.

3. ***Moderately impaired***
   Has one or more illness or disabilities which are either painful or which require substantial medical treatment.

4. ***Severely impaired***
   Has one or more illnesses or disabilities which are either severely painful or life threatening, or which require extensive medical treatment.

Table 5.2: Physical Health

Age Group	Good	Mildly Impaired	Moderately Impaired	Severely Impaired	Total
65 - 74	235 (54%)	184 (43%)	12 (2.8%)	1 (0.2%)	432 (100%)
75 & above	88 (49%)	69 (38%)	15 (8.5%)	8 (4.5%)	180 (100%)
Total	323 (53%)	253 (41%)	27 (4%)	9 (2%)	612 (100%)

The disabilities of the 253 elderly with mild impairment in physical health were:

		Frequency of cases
1.	Musculo-skeletal disorder e.g. arthritis, myalgia	20%
2.	Vision or hearing problem	15%
3.	Cardiovascular disorder e.g. hypertension, heart disease	12%
4.	Diabetes mellitus	9%
5.	Respiratory disorder e.g. bronchitis	3%
6.	Gastritis or Peptic Ulcer	2%

The disabilities of the 36 elderly with moderate or severe impairment in physical health were:

		Number of cases
1.	Stroke	15
2.	Heart diseases	8
3.	Arthritis	4
4.	Cancer	4
5.	Renal failure	2
6.	Chronic bronchitis	2
7.	Parkinson's disease	1

In general, most of the elderly in the survey were in satisfactory physical health — 53% had no significant illness and 41% had only minor disabilities. Only 6%, mainly in the older age group, had one or more major disabilities like stroke, heart disease, cancer etc. Mobility difficulty was found in only 8% of the sample and mainly in the old-old. Elderly patients unlike the young, tend to have multiple pathologies and this may cause treatment to be more problematic. Surveys in the United Kingdom and the United States concurred with the above findings that conditions most likely to limit functional ability among elderly people were heart diseases, arthritis and visual defects (Bond and Carstairs 1982, US Department of Health and Human Services 1987). The chronic illnesses affect the ability to perform tasks of daily living, quality of life, social roles, family relationship and emotional well-being.

As discussed before, there is a growing concern about caring for an increasing number of the frail elderly in Singapore. Traditionally, carers are the women in the family but because of the social transformation in the Singapore family, the traditional role of the family should not be taken for granted. Women are better educated now and prefer to go out to work rather than to remain at home. Another factor is the decrease in family size — most families today have only two children. The problem is further exacerbated by the disintegration of the extended family system as young couples tend to live away from their parents, because of employment or the constraint of space in high-rise apartments.

In a study of psychological distress in 60 principal family carers of elderly patients in the Singapore General Hospital, it was noted that 20% experienced symptoms of anxiety and depression (Kua 1989). There are social as well as psychological consequence of caring for a disabled or sick relative. Sanford (1975) reported anxiety and depression in 32% of carers. Psychological distress is often not associated with severity of disabilities of the patients. But those carers who lacked social support have a greater propensity to develop psychiatric symptoms. In the survey, most of the carers lived alone with the elderly relatives and were socially isolated. Many of them were also ignorant of the available services for the elderly in their community. Families in Singapore prefer to seek help either from relatives or close friends and are reluctant to request assistance from governmental agencies. Although there are only a few old people's homes or day centres in Singapore, families may not be eager to use these services because to send an elderly relative to these centres would imply a failure of family responsibility. However, with the change in family structure, many carers may have to turn to the community services for assistance. It is likely that in future the burden of caring for the majority of the frail elderly in Singapore will continue to rest on the family. Most families are unwilling to send their elderly to an institution — if it is done it is only as a last resort. Often for the very ill or disabled there is no alternative except for a home or hospital.

Although geriatric services in the community in Singapore are still limited, often such services are not known to patients or their relatives. In this study it was found that five families with stroke patients did not know that the Apex Day Care Centre, which is near their flats, provides stroke rehabilitation. The elderly were also asked whom they would consult if they had a minor ailment, e.g. fever. About 59% would seek medical advice from the general practitioners, 27% government clinics, 5% traditional healers or 'sinseh' and 9% self medication. This shows that the general practitioner plays a major role in the provision of geriatric care in the community. Some of the elderly prefered traditional healers or self medication because they felt that it was too costly to see a doctor. Government clinics are less expensive but are usually further away from their home. It is more convenient to go to the clinic 'downstairs' and see the family doctor whom they have established a good rapport over the years. Therefore, general practitioners should have basic knowledge of geriatric medicine through continuing medical education; and more importantly, a strong foundation from the undergraduate medical training programme in the University.

Supporting the carers with other community service programmes could include domiciliary nursing care, meals-on-wheel, befrienders' club, family carers' group and respite care. Expanding these services and making them accessible to those who need them, is crucial. Finally, health promotion and encouraging healthy lifestyle, e.g. exercises, nutrition, etc., are important strategies to prevent or minimise disabilities in late life.

6

DRINKING HABITS

Drinking is not uncommon amongst the Chinese, but it has been observed that the prevalence of 'alcoholism' is low. There have been suggestions that genetic predisposition may account for the low prevalence. The physiological reaction of flushing due to the autonomic sensitivity has been cited as a possible explanation (Wolff 1973, Reed *et al.*, 1976). Barnett (1955) reported that the Chinese in New York rarely developed 'alcoholism'. However, in a study of drinking habits of Chinese in Hong Kong, Singer (1972) refuted the notion that 'alcoholism' is rare. Environmental factors certainly influence attitude and alcohol consumption will certainly be influenced by the prevailing norm of the community. A study of the drinking behaviour of Chinese in downtown New York cannot be generalised to Chinese everywhere. The other important issue is the concept of 'alcoholism'. The ambiguity of this concept has led to confusion about what it really means. The crux of the matter is that in the past, 'alcoholism' tended to be defined in terms of severe dependence on alcohol. The misconception is that 'alcoholism' is the sickness of the 'alcoholic', who is the down-and-out drunk. Many patients may have alcohol-related problems without being dependent and are therefore not considered to have 'alcoholism'. If the incidence of a drinking problem is measured by the number of cases of 'alcoholism', then it is certainly low. To provide better understanding, it is more appropriate now to talk about the alcohol dependence syndrome (Edwards and Gross 1976) and alcohol-related disabilities.

In alcohol dependence syndrome, the person has to drink regularly and when he stops, after 8 to ten hours, he develops withdrawal symptoms of tremor, sweating and nausea. Drinking takes priority over all other things in his life and he feels a constant urge or compulsion to take alcohol. Moreover he finds that to achieve the same desired effect he needs to drink more than he used to. The alcohol-related disabilities include gastritis, peptic ulcer, liver diseases, head injury, fits, hypertension, diabetes mellitus, nerve disorders, poor memory, depression, hallucination, anxiety, family conflict (battered wife, divorce, child abuse), work problems (absenteeism, accidents, unemployment) and legal problems (drunken driving, disorderly behaviour, assault).

Currently, all studies on drinking in elderly people have been conducted in western countries. Traditionally, most Chinese prefer tea and there is an insistence on proper occasions for drinking alcohol like in weddings, festivals or birthdays. It is a rare sight to meet an inebriate in a Chinese community. However with the growing affluence of the newly industrialised countries like Hong Kong, Taiwan and Singapore, there is a tendency towards an increase in alcohol consumption. In the general hospital study of drinking problems in Singapore, it has been observed that almost all the cases were below 65 years (Kua 1986, 1987b). Is drinking problem uncommon in elderly Chinese?

In the GMS schedule there are questions on drinking behaviour but they tend to focus mainly on severe alcohol problems. In the survey, the subjects were also asked about their frequency of drinking, types of alcohol, quantity and alcohol-related disabilities. The spouses or care-givers were interviewed to provide a corroborative history. Those who drank more than once a week were requested to fill in the Severity of Alcohol Dependence Questionnaire or SADQ (Stockwell *et al.* 1979, 1983).

Table 6.1: Drinking Habits of the Sample
(in percentage)

Number of times per month	65-74 (n=432)	75+ (n=180)	Men (n=278)	Women (n=334)
Never drank	24	13	9	28
Less than once	36	14	18	32
1 - 3	7	3	8	2
4 or more	3	-	3	-
Total	100%		100%	

The majority of the sample (87%) either never drank or drank less than once a month (Table 6.1). About 10% drank once to three times a month. Those who consumed once or more times a week were the young-old men — only 20 subjects (3%). Their popular drinks were beer, stout or Chinese wine. Brandy was consumed on special occasions but other spirits like whisky or rum were less preferred. Eighteen subjects drank once or twice a week with a weekly average consumption of about 6 units (range 4-10) of alcohol; the other two drank three or more times a week with a weekly average consumption of 12 units of alcohol. Of the 18 subjects, two men had gastritis, and the mean SADQ score of this group was 4.2. The two subjects with the highest alcohol consumption, had symptoms of mild alcohol dependence and their SADQ scores were 10 and 12. Both of them had been drinking for about 18 years and their families mentioned that they tended to be abusive after drinking but did not appear to have any alcohol-related physical disabilities. The prevalence of alcohol dependence in this sample was estimated as 0.3%. With the inclusion of the two subjects with alcohol-related gastritis, the prevalence of drinking problems would be 0.6%.

Most studies in the west concur in their findings that alcohol-related problems are less prevalent among the elderly than among younger age-groups. Holzer *et al.* (1984) in the United States reported rates of alcohol abuse in men under 40 years as over 10%, but less than 5% in men over 60 years and below 1% in older women. In Scotland, Dight's survey (1976) showed that only 43% of men and 22% of women aged 65 and over were regular drinkers compared with 74% and 46% of the total male and female populations respectively. Compared with western countries in general, alcohol consumption in elderly Chinese is low both in frequency and quantity. Those elderly who drank regularly (at least once a week) comprised only 3% of the sample and there was no regular female drinker.

7

THE OLD-OLD

A salient point in Chapter 5 is that the physical health of elderly people between 65 to 74 years was generally good, and serious impairment was observed mainly in those 75 years and more. The 11-countries survey in Europe by the World Health Organisation, also confirms that change in health status becomes more dramatic after 75 years (WHO 1983). With a similar scenario in Singapore, it is imperative that gerontological research should focus more on this vulnerable group. It has been discussed previously that with the ageing of the population in Singapore, there is a proportional increase of the old-old and a decrease of the young-old.

Understanding the functional status of the elderly can provide valuable information on the elderly 'at risk'. The 'at risk' elderly are those who are frail and lack social or economic resources. They are at risk of neglect, deterioration of health, depression and suicidal tendency. The concept of functional status is wide, and although there are differences between countries on what to assess, the focus of interest is on health, economics and social support. Functional status is a measure of independent living in the community and assessment has been conducted using various schedules, namely: the Older American Resources and Services (Duke OARS 1978) the Comprehensive Assessment and Referral Evaluation (Gurland 1977) and the Philadelphia Geriatric Centre Multilevel Assessment (Lawton 1982). The OARS was used in this research mainly because of its holistic approach in assessment.

There were 180 elderly subjects aged 75 years and more, with 69 men (38%) and 111 women (62%) in the survey. They were subdivided into two age groups: (i) 75-79 and (ii) 80 & above. As shown in Table 7.1, in the younger group, there were 113 subjects with 41 men (36%) and 72 women (64%). In the older group, there were 67 subjects with 28 men (42%) and 39 women (58%). In marital status, 69% of the older group were widowed compared to 49% of the younger. However there was a higher proportion of singles in the younger group (11%) than the older group (6%). The majority of subjects in both groups were living with their family; 14% of the younger group were living with friends compared to 9% of the older group; and 8% of the younger group and 6% of the older group were living by themselves. In the report on the national survey of senior citizens (Ministry of Social Affairs 1983), about 84% of those 75 years & above, were living with their families and only 8% lived alone. Similarly in this study only a small proportion of the sample was living alone — 8% in the 75 to 79 group and 4% in the 80 years & above group. Those living alone were either single or widowed.

Table 7.1 Characteristics of the Old-Old

	Age Group	
	75 - 79 n=113 (100%)	80 & above n=67 (100%)
Sex		
Men	41 (36%)	28 (42%)
Women	72 (64%)	39 (58%)
Marital Status		
Widowed	55 (49%)	46 (69%)
Married	43 (38%)	17 (25%)
Divorced	2 (2%)	-
Single	13 (11%)	4 (6%)
Living Arrangement		
With family	88 (78%)	57 (85%)
With friend	16 (14%)	6 (9%)
Alone	9 (8%)	4 (6%)

The social resources rating scale assesses social relationships of the elderly person and whether help is available if needed. In the 75-79 age group, 80 subjects (71%) had good or mild impairment of social resources; and only 33 (29%) indicated moderate or severe impairment. In the 80 years & above group, 52 (78%) were generally satisfied with their social resources; and only 15 (22%) expressed dissatisfaction (Table

7.2). In the national survey of senior citizens, 53% of women and 44% of men, 75 years & above, said that they had no close friends; and only 70% had visits from children living apart from them.

Table 7.2: Functional Status of the Old-Old

	75-79 n=113 (100%)	80 & above n=67 (100%)
Social Resources		
Good or mild impairment	80 (71%)	52 (78%)
Moderate or severe impairment	33 (29%)	15 (22%)
Activities of Daily Living		
Good or mild impairment	103 (91%)	51 (76%)
Moderate or severe impairment	10 (9%)	16 (24%)

The performance rating scale of ADL is a measure of health and independence. In the younger age group, 103 (91%) had good or mild impairment of ADL; and only 10 (9%) were moderately or severely impaired. In the older group, 51 (76%) had good or mild impairment of ADL; and 16 (24%) had moderate or severe impairment. Comparing the two groups, the older group was more impaired in ADL ($p < 0.001$). All those with moderate or severe impairment had physical or mental disorders, e.g. stroke, cancer, chronic bronchitis, renal failure, heart diseases, depressive disorder and dementia. The results are comparable to the WHO (1983) sociomedical survey of the elderly in developed countries.

Table 7.3 is a cross-tabulation of social resources and activities of daily living of the 180 subjects. It can be seen that there were only three (2%) elderly who had moderate/severe impairment in both social resources and activities of daily living. They were the elderly who were unwell and lacked help — in short, the elderly 'at risk'. The importance of the functional status assessment is to identify the elderly 'at risk' and to plan services to meet their needs. Theoretically, the 'at risk' elderly are those who are disabled and living alone with poor social support. As mentioned from the outset, another dimension of enormous importance but not surveyed is the financial resources of the subjects. A more comprehensive assessment should certainly include this factor.

Table 7.3: Social Resources and ADL of the Old-Old

ADL	Social Resources Good/mild impairment	Moderate/severe impairment	Total
Good/mild impairment	109 (60%)	23 (13%)	132 (73%)
Moderate/severe impairment	45 (25%)	3 (2%)	48 (27%)
Total	154 (85%)	26 (15%)	180 (100%)

From the existing data it is possible to estimate, with caution, that for every 100 elderly (75 years & more) in the three constituencies, there are two 'at risk'. The rate should not be extrapolated to all other constituencies and may even be lower in future because the proportion of the healthy elderly will increase with improvement in health care. Better social support services in the community will also certainly reduce the rate. Therefore improvement in these two factors will diminish the number of 'at risk' elderly. One of the main objectives of the geriatric service is to provide assistance for the elderly 'at risk'. The array of essential services has been discussed in the Report of the Advisory Council on the Aged (Ministry of Social Affairs 1983). This network encompasses day care centre, in-patient hospital service, domiciliary care, home help, respite service, long-term care, etc. Identifying the elderly 'at risk' from a community survey is extremely exacting. A more rational approach is to maintain a register at primary health clinics and hospitals, of those frail elderly, who live alone, have financial difficulties or inadequate social support. The register will help the geriatric service to monitor and assist these elderly.

8

ELDERLY MEN AND WOMEN

Demographic statistics of most countries have consistently indicated that the life expectancy of women is higher than men. In Singapore today, the life expectancy of women is 74 years and men 72 years. In the United State women live about 7 years longer than men, the life expectancy of newborn girls is 79 years and boys 72 years. It has been theorised that this difference may indeed be genetically determined. Men are often the victims of major killer diseases like heart disease, stroke and cancer. Lifestyle contributes to the greater susceptibility of men. Women drink and smoke less than men and are less exposed to industrial pollutants or hazards. However some gerontologists have suggested that women tend to age faster psychologically. This is because most cultures place a high premium on youth and beauty, and women may feel that the menopause heralds the onset of ageing.

In the sample there was a slight preponderance of women (55%) over men (45%). This is similar to the 1980 census of population (Table 8.1). The sex ratio was almost similar in the young-old but in the old-old the ratio was 2 men : 3 women.

Table 8.1: Sex Distribution of Sample

	1980 Census	Sample
Men	51 200 (45%)	278 (45%)
Women	62 700 (55%)	334 (55%)
Total	113 900 (100%)	612 (100%)

The marital status of elderly men and women is illustrated in Table 8.2. It can be seen that 74% of men were married and 19% widowed, in contrast only 27% of women were married and 62% widowed. This may be because men tend to marry younger women and in old age they still have their wives around; but for elderly women, many of their husbands would have passed away. Moreover it is easier for a widower to remarry than for a widow. The main carers of elderly men were spouses (71%), sons (15%) and others (14%); but for women they were sons (31%), spouses (28%), daughters (23%) and others (18%). This shows that the elderly men relied more on their spouses but not elderly women. In living arrangement, 90% of elderly men lived with their families (spouses or children), 5% with friends and 5% alone. About 80% of women lived with their families, 14% with friends and 6% alone. Comparing the two groups, men tended to have better social resources — they had at least one person to take care of them indefinitely or for a short while.

Table 8.2: Characteristics of Elderly Men and Women
(in percentage)

	Men (n=278) 100%	Women (n=324) 100%
Marital Status		
Married	74	27
Widowed	19	62
Divorced	1	2
Single	6	9
Occupational Status		
Retired	77	45
Housework	5	44
Employed		
Part-time	6	2
Full-time	12	9
Physical Health		
Good	59	50
Mild impairment	38	45
Moderate or severe impairment	3	5

In occupational status, the majority of men (77%) were retired and 18% were still at work (6% part-time and 12% full time). Although 89% women were not working, only 45% mentioned that they had fully retired but 44% were still in charge of housework. About 11% of elderly women were still working—2% part-time and 9% full-time. Most elderly women continue to have a role status at home but some men may have problems adjusting to their role at home after retirement. An elderly woman remarked, "There should only be one person in the kitchen—two means friction." As discussed in Chapter 3, most of the elderly were employed as shop assistants or clerks and they were mainly the young-old.

Analysis of physical health status of elderly men and women (Table 8.2) does not show any difference between the two groups. The majority of men (59%) and women (50%) were in good health with no problems in activities of daily living. About 38% of men and 45% women suffered from mild disabilities like arthritis, diabetes mellitus, hypertension, etc. Only 3% of men and 5% women had moderate to severe illnesses, e.g. heart failure, stroke, cancer, etc. In mental health assessment, the prevalence of Alzheimer's disease was higher in women (1.5%) than men (0.7%) and the prevalence of multi-infarct dementia was 0.7% for men and 0.6% for women. For depressive disorder, women had a higher rate of 5.4% compared with men (3.6%). The data imply that elderly women have more physical and mental disorders but this must not be accepted at face value because there are more women in the old-old age group, which is a more vulnerable period for health problems. Because more elderly women never worked outside the home, they are financially dependant on their husbands or children.

9

THE ELDERLY IN SINGAPORE AND THE UNITED STATES

There are intriguing issues in comparative gerontology about differences and similarities in cross-national research on ageing. It is undeniable that cultural factor determines variation in perception of old age, and societal attitude influences how old people are cared in different communities. The aspiration and expectation of the elderly Americans are evidently different from that of the elderly Singaporeans. Beyond attitudinal and behavioural differences, what about health status and social support systems? Comparative gerontology is often plagued by variation in research methodology, questionnaire and rating scale. Any plausible conclusion becomes less cogent if there are ambiguities in the definition of the elderly, selection of sample or the questionnaire used. Most cross-national studies are not without methodological problems. The World Health Organisation multi-site study on dementia which involves developing and developed countries, has attempted to minimise the shortcomings by adopting a standardised interview instrument, the Geriatric Mental State schedule, and providing guidelines in the methodology of the survey. The study is still in progress and has the participation of over 10 countries including Singapore.

As mentioned previously, some sections of the questionnaire in this study were derived from the interview schedule of the Older American Resources and Services (Duke OARS 1978). This is a multi-dimensional functional assessment constructed by the Centre for the Study of Aging and Human Development, Duke University Medical Center, Durham, North Carolina. In the community survey in Durham county (Blazer 1978), a random sample of 10% of elderly residents aged 65 and over (n=997) was interviewed. Durham county is described by the author as "of rural orientation" and in contrast, the Singapore setting is urban. The demographic characteristics of the Durham and Singapore samples are seen in Table 9.1. They appear quite similar in age groups distribution.

The Elderly in Singapore and the United States

There is a preponderance of women in both groups and the difference is more marked in the Durham sample.

Table 9.1: Demographic Characteristics
(in percentage)

	Durham (n=997)	Singapore (n=612)
Age Group		
75 - 74	68	71
75+	32	29
Sex		
Men	37	45
Women	63	55
Marital Status		
Married	44	49
Widowed	46	42
Single	5	8
Divorced	5	9

Both the samples are compared on two parameters of functional status, namely activities of daily living (ADL) and social resources (Table 9.2). Performance of ADL is to a large extent a summation of physical and mental health. The two samples do not show major differences in the categories of ADL, except in severe impairment where the Durham sample has a higher frequency of 6% compared to the Singapore sample of 2% but the difference is not significant. However it must not be misconstrued that the Singapore elderly are healthier because the Durham survey was conducted 10 years earlier. But it does emphasise the fact the majority of elderly people in both cultures (over 60%) have good ADL. The health status of the Singapore elderly will follow the trend in the United States where there is high life expectancy and high proportion of healthy elderly.

Table 9.2: Comparison of Functional Status of Durham (D) and Singapore (S) Elderly
(in percentage)

Rating	Activities of Daily Living Durham	Singapore	Social Resources Durham	Singapore
Good	64	63	70	62
Mild or moderate impairment	30	35	25	29
Severe impairment	6	2	5	9
Total	100%	100%	100%	100%

In this study, 90% of elderly Chinese men lived with their family, 5% with friends and 5% alone. In the 1986 US census report, 82.5% of elderly American men lived with their family, 2.5% with friends and 15% alone. Elderly American women however had a different living arrangement — 56.5% with family, 2.2% with friends and 41.3% alone, in contrast to elderly Chinese women — 80% with family, 14% with friends and only 6% alone.

In social resources, a slightly higher proportion of the Singapore sample had impairment of mild, moderate or severe degree. This is surprising because there is apparently greater cohesiveness in family life in Singapore. Although more of the American elderly live alone, but they do have an array of community support services, e.g. meals-on-wheels, community nurses, physiotherapists, day centres, befrienders, etc. Even a widow living by herself with minimal family help can have good social resources if the available community geriatric services are readily at her disposal. In Singapore there is greater reliance on the family than on community support.

In the 1981 Harris poll in the United States, it was reported that 80% of elderly people mentioned they were satisfied with what they had achieved in life. Their main concerns were energy cost, crime, health and finance. In Singapore, 72% of the elderly Chinese expressed satisfaction with their life achievement. Their main concerns were health, finance and family relationship. It is interesting that the two groups are similar in their concerns about failing health and escalating costs. There is however a cultural difference in that the elderly Chinese were more family-oriented, and more affected by family conflict than the American elderly people.

In summary, the Singapore elderly is not too different from the American elderly in their ability to maintain independent living. Given the vigour of the national health campaigns, there will be a higher proportion of healthy young-old and old-old. What the American elderly lack in family support is compensated by good community-based services. With the social transformation of the Singapore family and consequent diminished family support, it may be necessary in the near future for families to seek more assistance from the network of services outside the home.

10

THE FUTURE ELDERLY

Old age is often viewed as the phase when decrements outweigh increments and skills deteriorate rather than improve. Societal perception of elderly people is often that of dependency and decay. As the French philosopher, Simone de Beauviour wrote, "The vast majority of mankind look upon the coming of old age with sorrow and rebellion. It fills them with more aversion than death." In the mass media old people are usually portrayed as frail and feeble. In times of economic woe, elderly people are deemed as a burden to society and a drain to the economy. Such prejudices arise from unfounded and unsubstantiated notions about old age, leading to systematic stereotyping and social discrimination.

This study has revealed some cogent data about elderly people in Singapore. The good news is that 53% of elderly people in the survey were in good health, 41% had minor ailments and only 6% were considered frail. The majority (90%) had no mental disorders and only 2% had dementia. About 94% were able to live independently and 14% were still working. The majority were not disgruntled about life in general and 72% expressed satisfaction. The compelling evidences should debunk the misconceptions about ageing. The improvement in health status and increase in life expectancy are good reasons for any nation to be exuberant — they are indices of Singapore's progress and should not be cause for dismay and disquiet. The resource potential of this burgeoning group is quite enormous — the challenge ahead is to galvanise the energy and capabilities of the healthy elderly. With the increase in life expectancy, there should be more good years to enjoy old age. In our youth we spend much time planning our career but unfortunately we tend to neglect planning for our old age.

It is estimated that one fifth of the population in Singapore will be 65 years and above in the year 2030. The configuration of the population pyramid would become more rectangular with time. The disconcerting statistics have given planners, economists and politicians the shudders.

But it will be these people and the baby boomers now in their thirties and forties, who are responsible for the alarming statistics. They are the cohort born after the Second World War, who will be the elderly boomers of the future. How different is this cohort from the elderly today? Firstly, they are better educated and probably more assertive. Secondly they are financially more secure and will be less dependent on their children. And thirdly, they are more health conscious and will be healthier. The present elderly are mainly poorly-educated and impoverished immigrants who have weathered the travails of poor nutrition, housing and health half a century ago. They have also survived the perils and ravages of war. But they laboured assiduously through an era when health insurance and Central Provident Funds were not introduced yet and many are not entitled to a pension. Will the cohort of baby boomers face difficult times in the future?

The pattern of disease will change with time. With the decline in mortality from infectious diseases and with healthy lifestyle, more people will survive to 65 or even 75. The prevalence of some diseases like heart illness or hypertension may be lowered, but others like Alzheimer's disease and cancer will be more common. Alzheimer's disease was rare in the past because people did not live long enough to be in that critical age when the disease would manifest. At present there is no preventive measure for Alzheimer's disease unlike multi-infarct dementia, which is related to hypertension and heart diseases. If social support diminishes, there may be a tendency for depressive disorder to increase among the frail elderly. But the elderly of the future will continue to enjoy many more years of good health. Today, young people have become more conscious about their diet and lifestyle. It can be expected that the majority of the future elderly will be active and fit. This has relevance to the human resource of the country — 30 years from now the retirement age may be 70 years and retiring at 60 or 65 will be an antiquated notion. With zero population growth, in many industrialised countries, the work force is shrinking and older workers have been persuaded to delay retirement.

Japan has adopted a flexible retirement age and a healthy worker can continue to work till 75 or more. The Japanese companies value the experience of mature workers. Regardless of age, people who see their job as meaningful, rewarding and like the job, tend to want to keep their job as long as possible. They may not be good for jobs that are too physically demanding or require speed, but their experiences compensate for slow speed and they can accomplish more in less time and with fewer mistakes. Given the opportunity, many elderly would prefer to work and they are a valuable resource. Well trained workers like teachers or nurses can be re-employed. The survey by JOICFP (1989) indicated that 42% of elderly Japanese worked "because it is good for health" and 39% "because of the income". Compulsory retirement grew along with industrialisation and growth of the corporation at the turn of the century. Age as the sole criterion for compulsory retirement is not valid because of the wide variations in the skills of elderly people. Flexible retirement would better utilise the skills and experience of the elderly. There is convincing evidence to show that life satisfaction and morale is better in older persons who are still working than those who have retired. With the anticipated change in retirement age, the old-dependency ratio has to be recomputed with the working age till 70 years or more to provide more realistic statistics. The old-dependency ratio is conventionally computed to examine the relative size of the elderly to that of the working age population. It is expressed as the ratio of persons 15-64 years of age to persons 65 years and over. In 1980, the ratio was 15:1 and in 2000 this will be reduced to 10:1, and 3:1 in 2030. The ratio will be less narrow if the retirement age is adjusted upwards with time and the statistics for 2030 will not be as forbidding as one elderly to be cared for by three working adults.

The lifestyle of the future elderly will certainly be different. Pre-retirement courses may be in vogue to prepare them for better financial security and occupy their leisure time with a myriad of recreational activities like sports, music, educational courses, art, etc. They may be seen more in clubhouses than in the community senior citizens' clubs, which will also cater for the more educated and well-heeled. Being financially more comfortable than the elderly today, they can afford to travel more often — the tour industry will certainly focus interest on this potential clientele. For those who missed university education in their youth, there may be opportunities to enrol in wide ranging courses, specially for matured students. In the developed countries today, such educational courses organised by tertiary institutions have been very popular among retirees. Many workers today who could not pursue a University education because of financial reason, may be able to fulfill an ambition. Most courses tailored for retirees are usually in arts or the basic sciences. The elderly of the future will also provide a vast potential market for the consumer industries. A whole catalogue of products ranging from clothing, appliances for the disabled, food, vitamins, magazine etc., will change the scene in supermarkets. Other business opportunities for the corporations include entertainment and insurance. In housing there appears to be a trend for the wealthy elderly to live on their own, away from their children. They prefer to live in small flats and have their children visit them on weekends. Telephone communication keeps them in contact with friends and relatives. This may be the perferred living arrangement for many families. In the United States, retirement communities or villages have sprung up in the recent years and provide facilities such as recreation, physiotherapy, nursing care, meals, group activities, etc..

The baby boomers are not only better educated and nourished, but are also imbued with an idealism different from their parents. They grew up in an era of relative social and political stability. But they have witnessed their counterparts in the West clamouring for a new social order. Because of their education, they tend to align themselves to the idealism of the West, though this idealism may be repressed as they pursue their individual careers. Today many of them have settled into comfortable positions in the establishment. It is unlikely that the idealism within their collective unconscious will remain dormant . It is gradually emerging as the baby boomers become more vocal and assertive. The growing number of elderly people in the future will invest them with enormous electoral power — they will be courted and wooed by political candidates. Invariably they will have a powerful lobby in the higher councils of government to champion their cause. But the idealism of the future elderly is different from that of the pugnacious youth demanding their rights. Their maturity and sagacity are assets, and as Dr Lin Yu Tang philosophised, "When a man grows old he develops a genious for flying low and idealism is tempered with cool, level-headed common-sense." They may petition for better services, needs and facilities, and certainly they cannot be ignored by any aspiring politician.

An issue of great exigency in the future is the care of the frail elderly, especially the old-old. The sole care provider at home will eventually be the spouse and the widowed or unmarried elderly may have to rely more on community services. Such services will ultimately be stretched very thinly and cannot provide comprehensive care. Reliance on private health services can be very exorbitant and health insurance will be a sine qua non. The wisdom of tapping the resources of the healthy young-old for community service has been discussed. It may be possible to inculcate neighbourhood spirit by encouraging the able-bodied elderly in a particular precinct to provide social support for the frail elderly there. The organisation of such self-help groups should be overseered by a committee in each housing estate. Basic health care training on nursing, physiotherapy and occupational therapy can be provided. Eventually such self-help group will continue to provide mutual support to succeeding generations of elderly people — such practice would eventually become the ethos of the community.

For the healthy young-old the range of voluntarism or part-time employment in the community may include day centres, homes, hospitals, hostels, library, schools, churches, club, etc. Such activities provide for mental stimulation, avert isolation and provide the elderly with a social role again. In the past, the elderly were the repository of knowledge in a community, but with modernisation and technological progress, their role has diminished; their children and grandchildren have also attained higher levels of education. Self esteem is usually a consequence of role status, which is often taken away on retirement. On this issue there is a gaping difference between the elderly in a rural and urban society.

Figure 10.1: Life Expectancy Curve and Projected Rectangularised Curve of Life Expectancy (The National Center for Health Statistics, USA)

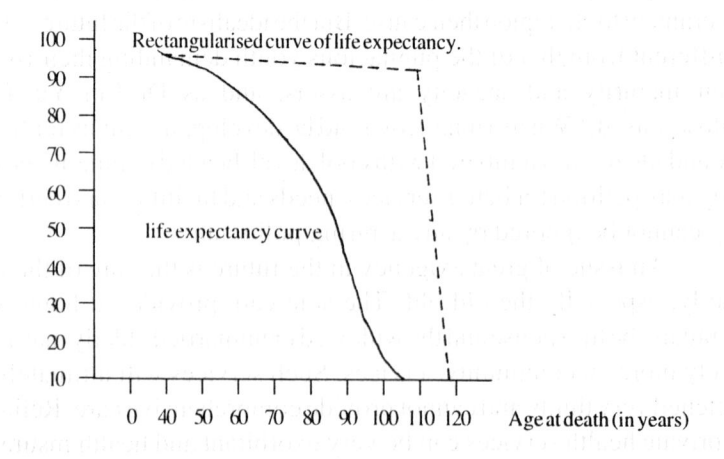

In the former the elderly assert greater control in an extended family and have a minor occupational status even on retirement. In the latter, there is less social stratification in the nuclear family and the crisis of role identity is more evident among retirees. The elderly in the rural community usually command a higher prestige.

The crucial issue in the ageing of the population is not the number of elderly people but the economics of the old dependency ratio and the care of the frail elderly. The dilemma of family carers has been discussed. The cost of health care of old people is now a major debate in the United States and western Europe. The elderly tend to have multiple illnesses and longer hospitalisation, and a greater proportion of their savings will be spent on health care. Various insurance schemes may be necessary to finance the escalating medical cost.

Illness in late life is inevitable but it is important to prevent early onset due to unhealthy lifestyle, e.g. obesity, lack of exercise, smoking and excess alcohol consumption. It is hoped that preventive medicine will allow life expectancy to be closer to life span. Lifespan refers to the biological limit of life — a maximum possibility of about 120 years. Life expectancy is the average length of time people can be expected to live — this is about 74 year in Singapore today for a newborn baby. The theoretical concept of the 'life rectangularisation curve' is shown in Figure 10.1. With the improvement of health and increase of life expectancy, elderly people could remain well for many more years and eventually succumb to a debilitating illness in the last few remaining months. In other words, the life expectancy curve follows the rectangularised curve of life. This would elevate the quality of life and also reduce health expenditure in the final phase.

The remarkable increase in lifespan means that we should appreciate old age and understand that elderly people can lead enjoyable lives. There is nothing depressing about growing old. We must not identify old age with imagery of decreptitude. The research has dispelled myths and misinformations, and provided a better insight about old age. At retirement, elderly people also need to seek new goals and roles to direct their energy and verve for a new sense of identity.

APPENDIX 1

The Elderly Cognitive Assessment Questionnaire (ECAQ)

Score 1 for correct answer

Memory

1. I want you to remember this number.
   Can you repeat after me (for example, 4517)? _____
   I shall be testing you again in 10 minutes
2. How old are you? _____
3. When is your birthday?
   or
   What year were you born? _____

Orientation and information

4. What is the day of the week today?
   What is the date today? _____
5.   day _____
6.   month _____
7.   year _____
8. What is this place called (for example clinic or hospital)?
   (It is not necessary to give the name of the place.) _____
9. What is his or her job (for example, nurse or doctor)? _____

Memory recall

10. Can you recall the number again? _____

                                             Total: _____

A brief questionnaire is needed to screen for cognitive impairment among elderly people in the community, clinic and hospital. The Elderly Cognitive Assessment Questionnaire is a 10-item scale and the items are culled from the Mini-Mental State (Folstein 1975) and the Geriatric Mental State Schedule (GMS). The ECAQ assesses 2 aspects of cognitive function, memory/orientation and information, and has a maximum score of 10 points. There is less bias on educational status and the questionnaire can be completed in less than 10 min.

      The validity of the ECAQ was compared with the Mental State

Appendix 1

Questionnaire or MSQ (Kahn *et al.* 1960). A nurse administered the ECAQ and MSQ to all the elderly people attending a day centre and an out-patient clinic. After that the subjects were assessed by the authors using the shortened version of the GMS. The data on the GMS were keyed into the computerized system, AGECAT, which could generate diagnostic syndromes. The validity coefficient of the ECAQ and MSQ are compared (Table 1). The sensitivity of the scales is similar but the ECAQ has a higher specificity and positive predictive value, and lower false-positive rate and overall miscalculation rate. In the ECAQ, a higher cut-off of 6/7 will attain a sensitivity of 100%, as all the cases have scores of 6 or less. But this will also include 17 false positives. The threshold score of 5/6 gives slightly better overall results than 6/7.

Table 1: Validity Coefficient of ECAQ and MSQ

ECAQ Cut-off point 5/6	Organic disorder (GMS-AGECAT)	
	Case (n-34)	Subcase/non-case (n=71)
Low score	29	6
High score	5	65
MSQ Cut-off point 7/8		
Low score	30	19
High score	4	52
	ECAQ	MSQ
Sensitivity	85.3%	88.2%
Specificity	91.5%	73.2%
Positive predictive value	82.8%	61.2%
False-positive rate	17.2%	30.8%
Overall miscalculation rate	10.5%	21.9%

As a brief scale, the ECAQ can be used by the busy general practitioner in the clinic for a quick mental status assessment, and also as a first-stage screening instrument in community surveys. In an epidemiological study of dementia in the community, there are a large number of normal respondents. A two-stage screening procedure is desirable in terms of cost-effectiveness and the interviewer's time. After the initial screening, potential cases can be confirmed by a subsequent diagnostic interview using a standardised questionnaire like the GMS.

REFERENCES

Anderson R (1987) "TheUnremitting Burden on Carers." *British Medical Journal*, 294:73-74.

Arie T & Jolley D (1982) Making Services Work: Organisation and Style of Psychogeriatric Services. In: *The psychiatry of Late Life,* Eds. Levy R & Post F. Blackwell, Oxford.

Arie T & Jolly D (1983) "The Rising Tide." *British Medical Journal*, 286:325-326.

Barnett, M L (1955) Alcoholism in the Cantonese of New York City, an anthropological study. In: *Etiology of Chronic Alcoholism*, Ed. Diethelm O. Charles C Thomas, Springfield.

Blazer OG (1978) The OARS Durham Surveys. In: *Multidimensional Functional Assessment - the OARS Methodology*, 2nd edition. Duke University Centre for the Study of Aging and Human Development, Durham, N.C.

Blazer D G (1980) The Epidemiology of Mental Illness in Late Life. In: *Handbook of Geriatric Psychiatry*, Eds. Busse E W & Blazer D. Van Nostrand Rheinhold, New York.

Blazer D G, Bachar J R & Manton K G (1986) "Suicide in Late Life." *Journal of the American Geriatric Society*, 34:519-525.

Blythe R (1972) *The View in Winter.* Penguin Books, London.

Bond J & Carstairs V (1982) Service for the elderly: a survey of the characteristics and needs of 5,000 old people. Edinburgh: Scottish Home and health Department.

Bowling A, Farquhar M & Browne P (1991)"Life satisfaction and association with social network and support variables in 3 samples of elderly people." *International Journal of Geriatric Psychiatry*, 6:549-566.

Census of Population (1980) Department of Statistics, Singapore. Singapore National Printers.

Chia B H (1981) *Suicidal Behaviour in Singapore*. SEAMIC. Tokyo.

Copeland J R M, Kelleher M J, Kellett J M, Gourlay A J, Gurland B J, Fleiss J L & Sharpe L (1976) "A semi-structured clinical interview for the assessement of diagnosis and mental state in the elderly: The Geriatric Mental State schedule. Development and reliability." *Psychological Medicine*, 6:439-449.

Copeland and J R M, Dewey M E & Griffith-Jones H M (1986) "Computerised psychiatric diagnostic system and case nomenclature for elderly subjects: GMS and AGECAT." *Psychological Medicine*, 16:88-89.

Copeland J R M, Dewey M E, Wood N, *et al.* (1987) "Range of mental illness among elderly in the community: Prevalence in Liverpool using the GMS-AGECAT package." *British Journal of Psychiatry*, 150:815-823.

Copeland J R M, Davidson I A, Dewey M E, *et al.* (1992) "Alzheimer's disease, other dementias, depression and pseudodementia: prevalence, incidence and 3 years outcome in Liverpool." *British Journal of Psychiatry*, 16:230-239.

Dight S (1976) "Scottish Drinking Habits: A survey of Scottish drinking habits and attitudes towards alcohol." *Office of Population Census and Surveys*, London.

Duke OARS (1978) *Multidimensional Functional Assessment: The OARS methodology*, 2nd edition. Duke University, Centre for the Study of Ageing and Human Development, Durham N.C.

References

Dukheim E (1951) "Suicide". Free Press of Glencoe, New York.

Edwards, G & Gross M M (1976) "Alcohol dependence: Provisional description of a clinical syndrome." *British Medical Journal*, 1:1058-61.

Folstein M F, Folstein S E, McHugh P R (1975) "Mini-mental state. A practical method for grading the cognitive state of patients for the clinician." *J Psychiatr Res.* 12:189-198.

Gilleard C J, Boyd W D & Watt G (1982) "Problems in caring for the elderly mentally infirm at home." *Archives of Gerontology and Geriatrics*, 1:151-158.

Gilleard C J, Gilleard E & Whittick J E (1984) "Impact of psychogeriatric day hospital care on the patients' family." *British Journal of Psychiatry*, 145:487-482.

Grahame P S (1984) "Schizophrenia in old age (late paraphrenia)." *British Journal of Psychiatry*, 145:493-495.

Gray B & Isaacs B (1979) *Care of the Elderly Mentally Infirm*. Tavistock Publication, London.

Greene J G & Timbury G C (1979) "A geriatric psychiatric day hospital service: A five year review." *Age and Ageing*, 8:49-53.

Gurland B J, Fleiss J L, Goldberg K, Sharpe L, Copeland JRM, Kelleher M J & Kellet J M (1976) "A semi-structured clinical interview for the assessment of diagnosis and mental state in the elderly. The geriatric mental state schedule. Factor analysis." *Psychological Medicine*, 6:451-459.

Gurland B J, Kuriansky J, Sharpe L, Simon R, Stiller P & Birkett P (1977) "The Comprehensive Assessment and Referral Evaluation (CARE) - Rationale, development and reliability." *International Journal of Aging and Human Development*, 8:9-42.

Gurland B J, Copeland J R M, Kelleher M J, *et al*. (1983) *The Mind and Mood of Ageing. The Mental Health Problems of the Community Elderly in New York and London.* Haworth Press 1983. London.

Harris, L (1981) *Ageing in the Eighties: America in Transition.* National Council on Aging. Washington DC.

Hasegawa K (1974) "Aspects of community mental health care of the elderly in Japan." *International Journal of Mental Health*, 8:36-49.

Henderson A S, Grayson D A, Scott R, Wilson J, Richwood D & Kay D W K (1986) "Social Support, dementia and depression among the elderly living in the Hobart community." *Psychological Medicine*, 16:378-390.

Henderson A S (1988) "The risk factors for Alzheimer's disease: A review and a hypothesis." *Acta Psychiatrica Scandinavica*, 78:257-275.

Holzer C E, Robins L N, Myers J K, Weissman W W, *et al.* (1984) Antecedents and Correlates of Alcohol Abuse and Dependence in the Elderly. In *Nature and Extent of Alcohol Problems among the Elderly.* Eds: G. Maddox, L N Robino & N Rosenburg. NIAAA, Washington DC.

JOICFP - Japanese Organisation for International Cooperation in Family Planning (1989). *Population Ageing in Asia.* JOICFP, Tokyo.

Jorm A F, Korten A E & Henderson A S (1987) "The prevalence of dementia: A quantitative integration of the literature." *Acta Pychiatrica Scandinavica*, 76:465-479.

Kahn R L, Goldfarb A L, Pollark M, Peck A. (1960) "Brief objective measures for the determination of mental status in the aged." *Am J Psychiatry*, 117:326-329.

Katon W (1984) "Depression: Relationship to somatization and chronic medical illness." *Journal of Clinical Psychiatry*, 45:4-11.

Katzman R (1986) "Alzheimer's Disease." *New England Journal of Medicine*, 314:964-973.

Kay D W K, Beamish P & Roth M (1964a) "Old age mental disorders in Newcastle upon-Tyne, Part I. A study of prevalence." *British Journal of Psychiatry*, 100:146-158.

Kay D W K, Beamish P & Roth M (1964b) "Old age mental disorders in Newcastle upon-Tyne, Part II A study of possible social and medical causes." *British Journal of Psychiatry*, 110:668-682.

Kay D W K, Henderson A S, Scott R, Wilson J, *et al.* (1985) "Dementia and depression among elderly living in the Hobart community: The effect of diagnostic criteria on the prevalence rates." *Psychological Medicine*, 15:771-788.

Kleinman A M (1982) "Neurasthenia and depression: A study of somatisation and culture in China." *Culture, Medicine and Psychiatry*, 117-190.

Koin D (1989) "The effects of caregiver stress on physical health status." In: *Alzheimer's Disease - Treatment and Family Stress*. Eds: Light E & Lebowitz B. National Institute of Mental Health, Rockville.

Kua E H, Tsoi W F, Chew S K, *et al.* (1983) "Mental Illness in the Elderly." *Singapore Medical Journal*, 24:6-10.

Kua E H & Tsoi W F (1985) "Suicide in the island of Singapore." *Acta Psychiatrica Scandinavica*, 7.1:227-229.

Kua E H (1986) "Alcohol-related hospitalisation in Singapore." *Singapore Medical Journal*, 27:392-399.

Kua E H (1987 a) "Psychiatric referrals of elderly patients in a General Hospital." *Annals Academy of Medicine*, 16:115-117.

Kua, E H (1987 b) "A cross-cultural study of alcohol dependence in Singapore." *British Journal of Addiction*, 82:868-870.

Kua E H (1989) "Psychological distress of carers of the frail elderly." *Singapore Medical Journal*, 30:42-44.

Kua E H & Ko S M (1992) "A cross cultural study of suicide in the elderly in Singapore." *British Journal of Psychiatry*.

Kua E H (1993 a) "Dementia in elderly Malays - preliminary findings of a community survey." *Singapore Medical Journal*, 34:26-28.

Kua E H (1993 b) "The depressed elderly Chinese living in the community: a 5-years follow up study." *International Journal of Geriatric Psychiatry*, 8:427-430.

Kua E H (1993 c) Prevalence of dementia in elderly Chinese and Malays in Singapore. Proceedings of the 4th Asean Congress on Psychiatry, Manila 1993.

Lawton M P (1982) "A research and service oriented multilevel assessment instrument." *Journal of Gerontology*, 37:91-99.

Lee S M (1987) *Spectrum of Chinese Culture*. Pelanduk Publication.

Li G, Shen Y C, Chen C H, *et al*. (1989) "An epidemiological survey of age-related dementia in an urban area of Beijing." *Acta Psychiatrica Scandinavica*, 79:557-563.

Lindesay J (1986) Suicide and attempted suicide in old age.In: *Affective Disorders in the Elderly*. Ed. E. Murphy Churchill. Livington, London.

Mahendra B (1985) "Depression and dementia: the multi-faceted relationship." *Psychological Medicine*, 15:227-236.

McClure G M (1987) "Suicide in England and Wales, 1975-1984." *British Journal of Psychiatry*, 150:309-314.

Miller M (1987) "Geriatric suicide: the Arizona study." *Gerontologist*, 18:152-158.

Ministry of Social Affairs (1983) *Report on the National Survey of Senior Citizens*. Ministry of Social Affairs, Singapore.

Ministry of Health (1984) *Report of the Committee on the Problems of the Aged*. Ministry of Health, Singapore.

Mortimer J A, Schuman K M & French L R (1981) Epidemiology of Dementing Illness. In: *The epidemiology of dementia*. Eds. Mortimer J A & Schuman L M. Oxford University Press, New York.

Murphy E (1982) "Social origin of depression in old age." *Brit J Psychiat*, 141:135-42.

Murphy E (1986) Social Factors in Depression. In: *Affective Disorders in the Elderly*. Ed. Murphy E. Churchill. Livingstone, Edinburgh.

Pahkala K (1990) "Social and environmental factors and depression in old age." *International Journal of Geriatric Psychiatry*, 5:99-113.

Parson PL (1962) "Mental health of Swansea's old folks." *British Journal of Preventive & Social Medicine*, 19:43-47.

Persson G (1980) "Prevalence of mental disorders in a 70 year old urban population." *Acta Psychiatrica Scandinavica*, 62:119-139.

Post F (1966) *Persistent Persecutory States of the Elderly*. Pergamon Press, Oxford.

Reed TF, Kalant H, Gibbons RJ, Kapur BM & Rankin JG (1976) "Alcohol and acetyldehyde metabolism in Caucasians, Chinese and Americans." *Canadian Medical Journal*, 5:851-855.

Roth M (1978) Epidemiological studies. In: *Alzheimer's Disease: Senile Dementia and Related Conditions*. Ed. Katzman R Raven Press, New York.

Sainsbury P (1955) *Suicide in London*. Chapman and Hall, London.

Sanford J R A (1975) "Tolerance of debility in elderly dependents by supporters at home: Its significance for hospital practice." *British Medical Journal*, 3:471-473.

Shibayama H, Kasahana Y & Kobayashi H (1986) "Prevalence of dementia in a Japanese elderly population." *Acta Psychiatrica Scandinavica*, 74:144-151.

Singer K (1972) "Drinking patterns and alcoholism in the Chinese." *British Journal of Addiction*, 67:3-14.

Stockwell T, Hodgson R, Edwards G, Taylor C & Rankin M (1979) "The development of a questionnaire to measure severity of alcohol dependence." *British Journal of Addiction*, 74:79-87.

Stockwell T, Murphy D & Hodgson R (1983) "The severity of alcohol dependence questionnaire: its use, reliability and validity." *British Journal of Addiction*, 78:145-55.

Teoh J I (1974) An analysis of completed suicide. *Annals of the Academy of Medicine*, 3:117-124.

Tseng W (1975) "The nature of somatic complaints among psychiatric patients: The Chinese case." *Comprehensive Psychiatry*, 16:237-245.

U.N. Department of International Economic and Social Affairs (1987) *Global Estimates and Projections of Population by Sex and Age.* United Nations, New York.

US Department of Health and Human Services (1987) Health Statistic on older persons. US DHHS. Hyattville, Md.

Victor C R (1987) *Old Age in Modern Society.* Croom Helm, London.

Whitlock F A (1979) "Suicide, Cancer and Depression." *Brit J Psychiat*, 132:269-74.

Wilson D R, Widmer R B, Cadoret R J (1982) "Somatic symptoms: a major feature of depression in a family practice." *Journal of Affective Disorder*, 5:199-207.

Wolff P H (1973) "Vasomotor sensitivity to alcohol in diverse mongloid population." *American Journal of Human Genetics*, 25:193-199.

World Health Organization (1978) *Mental Disorders Glossary and guide to their Classification in Accordance with the Ninth Revision of the International Classification of Disorders.* World Health Organisation, Geneva.

World Health Organisation (1983) *Public Health in Europe. The Elderly in Eleven Countries.* World Health Organisation, Geneva.

Yap P M (1965) Phenomenology of Affective Disorders in Chinese and Other Cultures. In: *Transcultural Psychiatry.* Eds. De Reuck AVS & Porter R J and A Churchill, London.

INDEX

Activity theory 14

Activities of daily living (ADL) 4, 7, 23, 24, 30, 34, 53, 54, 57, 59

AGECAT 27, 28, 30, 32, 33, 69

Ageing normal 26, 27

Ageism 43

Alcohol dependence 48, 50

Alcohol related disabilities 48, 50

Alzheimer's Disease 26, 28, 29, 30, 32, 57, 63

Anxiety disorder 38, 39, 46

Apex Day Centre 6, 47

Baby boomers 63, 65

Beijing 31, 32

Bukit Merah 4, 5, 6, 11

Carers 23, 30, 31, 40, 46, 47

Chinatown 5, 10, 11

Copeland 7, 27, 28, 32, 38, 39, 40

Clan association 21

Day centre 6, 40, 41, 42, 46, 54

Dementia 23, 26, 28, 29, 30, 31, 32, 41

Depression 26, 28, 33, 35, 37, 38, 46

Depressive disorder 32, 33, 34, 42, 57

Disengagement theory 14

Drinking 48, 49, 50

Durkheim 38

Durham 1, 58–60

Elderly Cognitive assessment Questionnaire 41, 68, 69, 70

Family support 15, 16, 17, 18, 35, 36

Forgetfulness 25, 26

Functional status 4, 51, 52

General practitioner 41, 47, 70

Geriatrician 41

Geriatric Mental State (GMS) 7, 27, 31, 32, 36, 49, 58, 69, 70

Geriatric services 47, 54

Index

Hasegawa 1, 29
Harris poll 60
Health assessment 6, 43, 44
Henderson 4, 5, 6, 11
Hobart 31, 35, 36

Immigrants 10, 11, 21
Intelligence 25
Intelligence test 25

Japan 1, 63, 64
JOICFP 64

Leisure activities 19, 20
Life satisfaction 13, 14, 61
Life expectancy 3, 55, 66, 67
Lifespan 67
Liverpool 31, 32, 38, 39, 40
Living arrangement 15, 52, 56
London 1, 31, 35, 36
Loneliness 18, 34

Malay elderly 16, 32, 37
Marital status 8, 9, 51, 52, 56, 59
Memory 25, 26, 68
Men
    dementia 32
    depression 33, 35
    elderly 4, 37, 38, 51, 55, 57

Mental health 4
Mental state assessment 7, 27
Mini-mental state 32, 68
Ministry of Social Affairs 3, 4, 20, 21, 52, 54
Mobility 45
Multi-infarct dementia 29, 30, 32, 57

National Registration Office 6
New York 1, 31, 34, 36, 48
Neurasthenia 37

Occupation 6, 22, 56, 57
Old-dependency ratio 64, 67
Older American Resources and Services (OARS) 1, 7, 15, 43, 51, 58
Old-old 2, 4, 8, 9, 16, 21, 24, 30, 33, 39, 43, 44, 51, 55

Paranoid 39
Paraphrenia 40
Perception of old age 4, 12
Performance skill 25
Physical health 4, 34, 35, 43, 44, 45, 56, 57
Population ageing 2, 62
Psychogeriatric services 40
Prevention 42

Religion 19, 20
Retirement 12, 13, 19, 43, 64, 67
Risk group 51, 54

Senescence 25, 26
Senile dementia 28
'Sin seh' 47
Sleep 27
Social class 5, 6, 9, 33, 34
Social isolation 30, 34
Social resources 4, 15, 16, 17, 33, 39, 52, 53, 54, 56, 60
Social support 4, 15, 16, 17, 18, 35, 42, 54, 63, 66
Somatisation 36, 37
Suicide 37, 38

Tiong Bahru 4, 5, 6, 11

UN Bureau of Census 1
United Kingdom 7, 20, 24, 41, 45
United States 7

Verbal skill 25
Voluntarism 20, 21, 66

Women
    dementia 32
    depression 33, 35
    elderly 4, 32, 38, 51, 55, 57
Working elderly 21, 22

Young-old 2, 3, 4, 8, 9, 16, 21, 24, 30, 33, 39, 43, 44, 51, 55